D1136216

EQUAL OPPOR
The Way Ahead

About Fullemploy
The Fullemploy group of companies aims to improve the economic base of minority ethnic communities through a partnership approach between the private, public and non-statutory sectors.
Fullemploy trains around 4,000 people each year in 17 centres in England and Wales, delivers race equality consultancy and produces tailor-made materials to aid organizations in implementing change in employment practices.

About the author
Jane Straw has worked for Fullemploy for the last four years, as trainer and adviser at one of their enterprize projects in Clerkenwell, North London, and as head of the central training, support and evaluation unit. She is now Managing Director of Fullemploy Publications Ltd. Previous experience includes an MA, work in publishing and several years spent freelancing in a wide variety of training, editing and writing roles.

About the contributors
Fitzroy Andrew is currently Head of personnel and staff development at Fullemploy Group Ltd. He has held a variety of personnel positions in local government, and supervisory and management positions in the private and public sectors.
After studying law at University College London, and spending several years freelancing and studying in Europe, Eton Morrison joined the Fullemploy organization as Information Officer in 1986. He has been active in the formulation and implementation of Fullemploy's positive action strategies, and has recently been made Policy Research Officer for Fullemploy Training.

EQUAL OPPORTUNITIES

The Way Ahead

Jane Straw

of Fullemploy

Institute of Personnel Management

First published 1989
Reprinted 1989

Phototypeset by Input Typesetting Ltd, London
and printed in Great Britain by
Short Run Press Ltd, Exeter, Devon.

British Library Cataloguing in Publication Data
Straw, Jane
    Equal opportunities: the way ahead.
    1. Great Britain. Employment. Equality of opportunity
    I. Title   II. Institute of Personnel Management
    331.13'3'0941

    ISBN 0-85292-422-4

Contents

Acknowledgements

This handbook has been a team effort in both conception and execution. Especial thanks must go to Fitzroy Andrew, Head of Personnel at Fullemploy, who contributed chapters 3 and 4 on the operation of equal opportunities in employment, and to Eton Morrison who put together chapter 2 on equal opportunity legislation. Thanks also to Tim Webb of MSF; and to Cherry Ehrlich of the BBC, Herman Ouseley of ILEA, Sue Field of Barclays and Peter Bassey of Littlewoods who gave a great deal of their time to chapter 6. Eulyniss Roberts and Marion O'Brien tirelessly typed and retyped and Daniel, Adam, Chloe and Ed got on with life without me being around too much. Final thanks go to Fullemploy, the provider of the active experience out of which much of this book has grown.

Chapter 1 Setting the scene

The importance of equality of opportunity in employment has never been more central to all of us involved in work, whether secretaries, personnel, senior management or chief executives.

In the past, with a plentiful workforce to draw upon, it has been an approach which some organizations have chosen to adopt as part of good professional personnel practice. Yet in the 1990s, against a background of demographical change, an understanding and practice of equal opportunities policies is essential if the UK is to meet the demands of an increasingly competitive market, and, indeed, if some organizations are to survive at all.

Equal Opportunities: the way ahead traces out the background to this scenario and the history of equal opportunities policies. It covers relevant legislation and the role of education and training, and focuses on how a selection of public and private sector organizations are already operating equal opportunity policies. It looks at what equal opportunity in employment practices means and suggests ways of introducing these policies into organizations. It looks at the way ahead: at likely legislative, economic and social changes which will inevitably affect us all in the next decade.

But first let us move for a moment beyond the solution and look at the problem itself.

Why haven't employment practices, including recruitment and promotion, always been equal? Many people would say they have. 'Look,' they may say, 'we have 50 per cent women in our firm' without pointing out that 48 per cent of those same women are below middle management grade. 'Oh well,' they may say, 'we have no minority ethnic people in senior positions but that's because they don't apply,' without looking at *why* they don't apply or, more relevantly, why, if they do apply, they don't get the job. Because, whether we recognize it or not, each one of us has and probably will feel prejudice, and discrimination is a result of that.

It is the recognition and the development of practices which will lessen its impact that this book attempts to address.

How prejudice occurs

Prejudice can develop for any reason – not necessarily through a strongly-held, recognized bias based on race or gender, although that happens as well – but often just because a mannerism or a remark is unfamiliar.

For instance, when you are walking down the street and see someone coming towards you, you form an impression of that person. That impression is based on a number of factors, including dress, hair, gender, way of moving and facial expression.

If that person is limping, or has only one arm, or is in a wheel-chair you will probably feel sympathy because they look as if they need help. If that person is female, of minority ethnic origin, dressed in an expensive suit and carrying a briefcase you may feel a combination of unease and possibly resentment because she is not fitting into your expectations. If that person is white, male, well-dressed and just about to get into a BMW, you may look at him with envy, but your expectations of him will not be challenged, nor will his right to do what he is doing.

Prejudice is often so difficult to spot in particular circumstances that those on the receiving end aren't sure whether it is really there.

For instance, a couple of months ago I was standing behind two female, Afro-Caribbean colleagues waiting to get off a train. In front of them was a white male. He quickly jumped off first and slammed the door in their faces. We looked at each other. Did he do it because he was in a hurry, because they were Afro-Caribbean, because they were women, or because *we* were women?

What we expect is based on our family, our education and our life experiences. Anything other than what we expect challenges our assumptions and makes us respond in a particular way. Difference breeds suspicion: if an individual looks and acts differently it takes an extra effort to feel comfortable being with them.

If this effort isn't made, the seeds of indirect discrimination are being sown, growing from the initial feelings of prejudice. We may not seem to be treating an individual less favourably because of their colour, their appearance or their gender. Indeed, we may be aware that this kind of direct discrimination is in many cases illegal (see chapter 2). We may even pride ourselves on being liberal and forward-thinking.

But when we wonder whether this well-qualified person in a wheelchair will be able to gain respect in a busy office and decide that she won't; when we feel that we can't promote the extremely able Muslim worker to supervisor because his staff will not be managed during his prayer-times and Ramadan; when we hold back from making the female junior manager into project leader, despite her outstanding ability, in case of accusations of favouring a young, attractive woman – then we are operating a policy of indirect discrimination. There are innumerable other examples.

A Commission for Racial Equality study carried out in 1987 entitled *Chartered Accountancy Training Contracts* looked at such discrimination in more depth in relation to minority ethnic recruitment into chartered accountancy. Its findings showed that different forms of discrimination can interact to block entry for a particular group into a profession.

The aim of the investigation was to discover whether the minority ethnic applicants were gaining access to this profession in proportion to their numbers in the relevant labour market – or the population as a whole.

Results of the study were as follows:

- application rates from black people varied from firm to firm

- minority ethnic trainees felt that the City, and the accountancy profession projected a 'white, male public-school image' and that few accountancy firms included people from different ethnic groups in their recruitment literature

- although the firms claimed that they selected on academic criteria, this was not consistently applied. Other factors such as the 'right chemistry' were taken into consideration – a potential opening for stereotyping.

- few interviewers at manager and partner level were aware of the ways their perceptions of people from another racial group could affect assessments, or of the misunderstandings which could result from different cultural responses

- few recognized that racial discrimination was part of the experience of an applicant from a different ethnic background

- no forms were used to monitor interview assessments or validate results against subsequent performance.

The CRE concluded that minority ethnic applicants were still rejected disproportionately at interviews. Reasons for this were:

1   the qualities looked for in the search for the successful candidate might be inappropriate for minority ethnic groups and women eg membership of clubs and societies, which does not necessarily indicate that the applicant has good social skills

2   the lack of awareness among interviewers of their own stereotyped view, and of the way in which their unconscious perceptions about people from another racial group might affect their assessments, might make them less able to judge the ability of minority ethnic candidates

3   the extent of these candidates' feelings of frustration, particularly associated with experiences of racial discrimination, which might affect their interview performance.

So where does this take us? Prejudice exists. It exists, inevitably, in each one of us. It can lead to both indirect and direct discrimination. Prejudice itself is not something to be punished for, except when it leads to breaking the law which, sadly, it often does. However because of its negative effects, both on an individual and on society, it is something to become aware of and to overcome, both for the good of the organization and its employees.

Different kinds of discrimination

Before we can move on to organizational practices, we need to look at the kinds of discrimination the different groups covered in this hand-book experience, because they grow from very different prejudices.

As part of this it is important to establish that each of the groups is in need of more equal employment policies **not** because of any lack of ability or potential, but because of past operation of discrimination in all of its forms.

Minority ethnic groups

Here, prejudice operates on the basis of race; the fact the skin is a different colour means that the person is *different*. The physiognomy will be different too. Hair may be strong, black and curly, bone structure more elongated, eyes larger, noses flatter. Language will either be totally different or, where entry to the UK has been relatively recent, intonation may recognizably belong to a particular racial group. Dress may be very different.

Where particular religions are followed, difference in holidays, in times of work, and in a belief system will be very obvious. Codes of behaviour, what to say, how to say it and food preferences will all vary from what is taken as the norm – from 'the way we have always done things round here'.

I recently went to a cookery demonstration which covered the preparation and eating of Caribbean food: yams, sweet potatoes, jerk chicken. The preparation was long and thorough; careful washing, cleaning, marinading and spicing, all as a matter of course. It explained why several of my Afro-Caribbean friends prefer not to eat at cafes or restaurants, through concern over hygiene and taste. It made me realize that my previous reaction to what I saw as their unreasonableness was taking it at face value rather than making an effort to understand.

To minority ethnic groups, who make up roughly five per cent of the population of the UK, such differences are important in terms of identity. How many times have you been in a room with people who are a different colour to you and have different accents? This is everyday experience for minority ethnic groups in this country, and retaining a sense of identity with their family, community and traditions is essential.

How do white people react to this complex and varied set of differences? We either embrace the need for adaptation and change or we resist it as potentially threatening. After all, exploring differences might call for a degree of self-analysis. In order to control the difference, a number of stereotyped responses develop: *it is not my concern* (I don't come into contact with many minority ethnic people), *exclusion* (keep away from me), *assimilation* (absorb the different identity into my culture), *humiliation* (different so not right), or *abuse*.

When these individual responses are transferred to organizations as the behaviour patterns of the people who make the decisions, then they become the conscious or unconscious basis of that organization's structure.

For instance, where the majority of senior management are white and male (still the situation in most organizations in the UK), the beliefs and culture of that organization will be predominantly white and male. An instance of this would be where a head of department is unable to see that a well-qualified minority ethnic woman could be his deputy. During the interview he may look for a variety of reasons why not: she may be going to have children, she won't want to work late, the rest of the department won't like it and then I'll have to sort it out, etc. This attitude will create a pattern in the department which will block the recruitment or promotion of most people who vary from the organization's accepted cultural norm.

Women

For women prejudice operates differently. For one thing there are more of them and also, everybody knows one! She may be your wife, mother or girlfriend, but it would be very difficult to get through life without some fairly regular contact with women.

So where does the problem lie? Well, first, with the situation in which women have traditionally been put. The majority are seen as mothers or wives, doing the cooking, making the beds, doing the shopping, taking responsibility for the domestic side of life. (It's worth stating that these are all important roles and where women are fulfilled in these roles, this book does not suggest they should become so guilty that they stop!)

Where expectations of women traditionally focus on the domestic, it is more difficult to envisage them in a work environment. Here, the personal and the professional are inextricably linked. Can the woman who washes your socks also take decisions on multi-million pounds budgets? Should the secretary who makes your coffee be given opportunities for development so that one day she will be able to do your job? And should *you*, as a male reader, be taking on more of a domestic, self-sufficient role so that these women can compete more effectively in employment?

The usual next step in response to this argument is 'Ah yes, but what about the children? Women have to take responsibility for the children because it's only natural. After all, they bear them.'

This argument can and has been debated widely. Whichever conclusion you come to, however, its effect is that in general women take responsibility for the day to day welfare of their children and are offered little support in terms of child care provision from either state or private sector. The effect of this is that they are perceived as part-time (i.e. part-time without the possibility of promotion) and unreliable (because of school holidays, sickness). The result of this is that the majority of women are caught in a cycle of low-paid, part-time work with little promotion beyond junior levels.

The combination of low expectations from themselves and others and poor child-care arrangements means the skills which women may have developed through domesticity and motherhood are ignored. These include skills in organizing, in forward-planning and budgeting and in interpersonal and communication skills.

For example, a young mother had returned to train as a P.A. after having children. During a mock interview to develop her interviewing skills she uncharacteristically mumbled and became silent when asked about a three year gap between jobs. In the feedback session I asked her why she seemed to have a problem with that particular question. 'Well that's when I had my child' she replied. Conditioned into seeing motherhood as offering nothing to the world of work, her usually vital and professional manner crumbled. She expected to be discriminated against.

It is not, however, only men who discriminate against women in employment. As the first women reach senior management positions, there is some evidence of women discriminating against other women. This may be based on the 'I had to work hard to get where I am so you should too' prejudice, and as a development of that 'I've succeeded in a man's world and I'm not sure I want other women to do so too', or more simply just an adoption of the prevailing man-made culture of an organization without challenging its assumptions.

The disabled
Prejudice against the disabled grows from other sources, primarily sympathy. A typical response when faced with a person with a visible physical disability is one of regret that the person isn't able to participate in the way an able-bodied person would be able to.

Another response is not to talk about the disability. Another response is to show great concern about the comfort of the disabled person and the facilities available to them, and a reluctance to ask them to do too much.

Where their disability is mental, there may be a greater degree of uncertainty about their abilities and a greater degree of fear of the unknown and of what to expect, which may limit what they are asked to do.

What all these responses add up to is low expectation of the individual which, despite the legislative minimum of three per cent of an organization's workforce needing to be registered disabled, leads to low recruitment and promotion prospects. The fact that the involvement of disabled people in the workforce often means an increase in expenditure in terms of facilities, equipment and human support is an additional factor, as is a concern about the effects and demands on other employees.

The kind of discrimination which grows from these factors means that disabled people have to try twice as hard to prove their abilities and capabilities to move past this blanket of sympathy. Where their disability is visible they may never manage to do so.

Older people

Prejudice against older people rests much more on the belief that certain skills and abilities have been lost, without being replaced by other qualities.

Where the culture of an organization puts an emphasis on youth and the qualities usually represented by it, this introduces an automatic cut-off point for those not classified as young. It is no surprise that in the UK the majority of recruitment advertisements specify an age limit of 40.

Yet whereas the perception is that energy, creativity, enthusiasm, determination and stamina diminish with age, the other side of the coin, that reliability, thoroughness, experience and patience will make up for these qualities where, indeed, they have lessened, is not there.

The result of this is that in-company training and promotion and external recruitment falls off rapidly after 40, and early retirement programmes come ever lower down the age scale. This kind of discrimination seems to be a British peculiarity. Top jobs in Germany are rarely filled by those under 40, and in other countries the wisdom and experience developed with age is given a top priority in filling a wide range of jobs.

These different forms of discrimination are likely to work to compound each other. For instance if you are a female, of minority ethnic origin and confined to a wheelchair you would arguably be at a greater disadvantage in the recruitment and promotion stakes than a white male over 45.

The impact of change

Although we've seen how prejudice and discrimination works and the different forms it can take we have not looked at why equal opportunity policies are necessary. There are a number of factors which have come together to make them more necessary than ever before. These include changes in the structure of employment, demographic changes, social and moral factors, and hard-nosed business necessity.

Structure of employment
The rapid change in the structure of employment which has brought about a need for a more varied and flexible workforce has affected both employers and employees alike and will continue to do so well into the next century.

This change includes a decline in manufacturing and a growth in service industries, with 300,000 new jobs in distribution and hotels, half a million in business services such as insurance and banking and 800,000 in miscellaneous services being the figures estimated for between 1986 and 1995.

It includes the continuing introduction of new technology, with an estimated need for a 25 per cent increase in professional information technology staff between 1985 and 1990.

It includes weakening job demarcations and changes in the organization of working practices, with an estimated increase of 1.27 million people in part-time jobs by 1995 and a rise of 500,000 in those becoming self-employed between 1986 and 1995. It is also estimated that there will be a fall in the length of the average working week for males from 42 hours at present to 34 hours by the year 2010.

The main outcome of this change is skill shortages and mis-

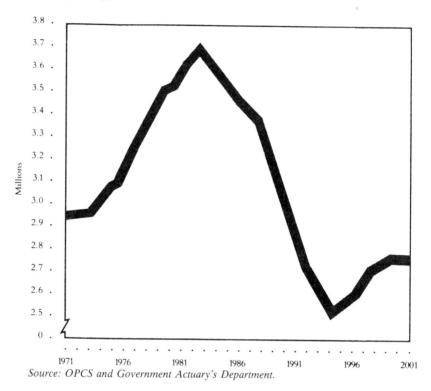

Source: OPCS and Government Actuary's Department.

Figure 1
Population aged 16–19 in Great Britain 1971–2001

matches as education and training struggle to adapt to new demands of the job market (see chapter 7). This in turn will affect productivity and the wealth of the country.

Demographic issues
Predictions into the 1990s suggest that the labour force will continue to grow but at a slower rate than in the mid-1980s. Between 1987 and 1995 the number of people in the labour force will increase by 100,000 a year compared with over 300,000 a year in the four years between 1983 and 1987. The numbers aged 16–19, however, will have fallen by over 1 million between 1983 and 1993, figure 1, a reduction of around 25 per cent, and the number

aged under 25 is projected to fall by 1.2 million between 1987 and 1995.

Within the main thrust of demographical changes different groups are affected in different ways. Women returning to the labour force after having children, for instance, will be a major target for employers. The number of women aged 25 to 44 in the workforce is expected to rise by 600,000 by 1995, a sizeable proportion of the total rise. This will exacerbate a trend which has already begun. Female employment has grown steadily since 1983, while male employment has declined. The levelling out of the 1970s baby boom will lead to women taking up 80 per cent of new jobs from 1995 onwards. This factor alone will necessitate more flexible working conditions and a change in approach to both recruitment and promotion for married women.

It is clear, however, that many employers underestimate the scale of the fall in the number of young people.

When the personnel divisions of 20 large organizations were interviewed between November 1987 and January 1988, only seven were aware that the decline in the number of school leavers would be 25 per cent.

These two factors – rapid change in the structure of employment and in demography – mean that it is essential for employers to develop flexible equal opportunity employment practices, with training and re-training packages available to all employees.

Social factors

The dramatic, immediate social results of discrimination have been given wide coverage in the press. The rise in feminism, inner city riots, racial harassment and physical abuse have all occupied the headline writers and media analysts in recent years.

This however makes up just one element of a much broader change in social fabric and attitudes which put different demands on the employing organization. This broader aspect includes changes in the structure of families, mobility patterns and expectations of work.

For instance, married women are being given greater opportunities to enter the workforce, due to demographic factors. 62 per cent of married women now work (General Household Survey 1980 – HMSO 1982) although over half of those are currently in part-time work. They will bring with them demands for improved childcare provision and flexible hours. The employers who respond to these demands will be better placed to retain the skilled workforce which they need.

Moral factors
There is a growing awareness of moral responsibility amongst organizations who recognize themselves as part of their local community. This brings with it a recognition of the need to bring prosperity to that community by providing employment, by building links with local schools and colleges and by feeding back into its development. For example where an organization is in a multiracial area with, say, 12 per cent of residents coming from minority ethnic groups, it may aim to reflect that 12 per cent in the composition of its workforce.

There is also the absolutely clear moral argument that discrimination is wrong and that equality of opportunity is the right of each individual. In employment terms a reluctance to operate equal opportunity policies means human wastage both for the individual and the organization.

Business reality
It is nevertheless a fact of life that in the past the moral argument has not been particularly effective in convincing employers of the need to introduce equal opportunity policies.

The overwhelming reason why these policies are now centre stage is because in the current climate outlined above *they make good business sense.*

Without them, employers are quite clearly going to experience problems in gaining and retaining a workforce. In the short-term the introduction of equal opportunity policies will make great demands on the organization, through time spent in planning and implementing, through personnel to carry out the policies, and the cost of funding their introduction and maintenance – record keeping, monitoring and wider based advertizing. And this is without work-place nurseries and crêches, training and re-training.

However unless this short-term view is overcome by the long-term perspective, then by the mid-1990s organizations which have not introduced equal opportunity policies will suffer employee shortages, skill shortages, low productivity and profitability. In comparison, those which have planned for the future and introduced equal opportunity policies as part of their professional practices should have secured a stable, well-trained, skilled workforce.

The individual and change

There is, however, another element in this equation, and that is the employee. Both potential and existing employees will need to examine their own strengths and ambitions and adjust them to a new labour market.

Their aspirations, their perceptions of themselves and of the sort of work they feel is appropriate or acceptable, will be influenced by their class, family, education and by the media.

For instance, a young Afro-Caribbean deciding on a career may reject the police force due to pressures from his or her peer group. In a different way he or she may not consider becoming a barrister, due to lack of encouragement in seeing the job as attainable. A woman may become a secretary without ever considering moving upwards to become a personal assistant, or may reject moving into the more specialized and highly paid information technology field because of a lack of confidence in her ability with machines.

There are many examples of conditioning leading to underfulfillment. Affecting the perceptions which each one of us brings to the labour market is a complex task but involves education, social beliefs, expectations and what meets us when we enter that market. For the process is interactive, in that employers will bring their own perception of what to expect from both potential and established employees based on their own background and experience. Once again, it's the example of the woman who washes socks also managing a multi-million pound budget.

Dual labour market economy

One result of low expectations from employees, discrimination by employers and a lack of flexible employment policies can be seen in the emergence of the dual labour market economy in the United States.

The dual labour market consists of two sectors: the primary and secondary sector. In the primary sector work is characterized by good working conditions and pay levels, career prospects and stability.

Secondary sector workers are characterized by considerable instability and a high turnover rate, low in-house training and poor promotion prospects. There is a high proportion of members of minority ethnic groups, women, unqualified teenagers, students seeking part-time work and disabled people.

In America, these secondary sector workers have developed into an 'underclass' of part-time, temporary, low-paid employees. The downwards spiral which accompanies this underclass includes extremes of poverty, poor educational achievement, poor housing, violence and crime – all linked to the removal of the right to reliable employment and income.

If we in the UK are to avoid this scenario, and there are elements of it already in some parts of the country, then the operation of equal opportunity policies which will draw women, the disabled and minority ethnic groups into the emerging mainstream employment opportunities is essential. In this sense these policies will become an agent of social change. Part-time work need not equal a lack of progression in career terms: a disabled employee need not only be offered simple tasks to do, members of minority ethnic groups should be perceived as chief executives and managers as well as secretaries and shop floor workers.

The essential nature of equal opportunity policies for the future, then, has been established. The framework within which employers will activate these policies includes recruiting from new or under-utilized sources, retraining their existing workforce and ensuring that their employment policies and practices are fair and flexible enough for them to attract and keep a relatively stable workforce.

In introducing and maintaining these policies three strands of management should act in tandem: *top management* to support and reinforce, *personnel management* – the source of the knowledge and planning needed to make the policies effective, (see Appendix I for the IPM's Equal Opportunities Code) – and *line management* which is pivotal in implementing the policies.

We shall be looking in detail at how equal opportunities policies can operate in subsequent chapters. The next chapter provides the legislative context both in Britain today and in Europe.

Chapter 2 Equal opportunities legislation

This chapter, as well as providing an overall survey of equal opportunities legislation, also aims to provide an appreciation of the effectiveness or otherwise of the various domestic legislative measures of recent years, and to show how these interact with EEC directives and regulations. This chapter will also examine the role played by the CRE, EOC and IPM in terms of supporting the legislative objectives and clarifying its provisions. Finally, for purposes of general comparison with the state of play in Britain, there will be a brief examination of how equal opportunities legislation has operated in other countries, particularly in the USA, as much of our domestic discrimination law has taken a lead from the American experience.

Summary

The following tables set out the major Acts of Parliament and EEC regulations and directives, sub-divided into the specific areas of equal opportunities activity encompassed by this book: race, women, disability, sexual orientation and age. What is immediately clear is that there has been little or no direct parliamentary action regarding discrimination on grounds of sexual orientation or on grounds of age. However, there are indications that these issues are increasingly coming to the attention of personnel practitioners and other professionals working in the field of equal opportunities, as well as gaining more attention in the media.

Table I

Race equality legislation	Brief description
1 Treaty of Rome 1957	this makes it unlawful to discriminate against EEC workers on grounds of nationality and citizenship.
2 Race Relations Act 1965	repealed by the RRA 1968. This Act made it unlawful to discriminate on grounds of colour, race, ethnic or national origins in places of public resort.
3 Race Relations Act 1968	repealed by the RRA 1976. This Act extended the 1965 Act into the areas of employment, provision of services and housing provision.
4 Race Relations Act 1976	this Act entirely replaces the RRA 1968 and is currently in force. The Act redefines discrimination to cover previous loop-holes and introduces the concept of 'indirect discrimination' to the area of race (based on Sex Discrimination Act 1975); the Act also establishes important exceptions such as 'positive action'. The Act also sets out the role of the Commission for Racial Equality (CRE).

Table II

Sex equality legislation	Brief description
1 Treaty of Rome 1957	Art. 119: 'Each Member State shall during the first stage ensure and subsequently maintain the application of principle that men and women should receive equal pay for equal work'.
2 Equal Pay Act 1970	this Act makes it unlawful to discriminate between men and

Table II—(Continued)

Sex equality legislation	Brief description
	women with regards to pay and other contractual terms and conditions.
3 Sex Discrimination Act 1975	the provisions of this Act apply equally to discrimination against either sex. However women are the major beneficiaries given the greater likelihood of their being subjected to unequal treatment on grounds of sex. The Act establishes two forms of discrimination, direct and indirect, both of which are unlawful. The Act also establishes the role of the Equal Opportunities Commission (EOC). The RRA 1976 was modelled on this Act.
4 Equal Pay (Amendment) Regulation 1983	these are amendments to the existing equal pay legislation brought about by proceedings against the British Government brought by the European Commission. The amendments made it possible to claim equal pay for work which is considered to be of 'equal value' to that done by a member of the opposite sex.
5 Sex Discrimination Act 1986	this Act introduces amendments bringing British sex discrimination law in line with the EEC Equal Treatment Directive (76/207/EEC). Major amendments affect discrimination in collective agreements, employment for the purposes of private households, employment in firms with five or fewer employees, and retirement ages.

Table II—(Continued)

Sex equality legislation	Brief description
6 Directive on Equal Pay (75/117/EEC)	this establishes that the principle of equal pay stated in Art. 119 Treaty of Rome (above) refers to work which is the same or which is judged to be of equal value, and requires the introduction by member states of the appropriate legal mechanisms for the redress of all discrimination on grounds of sex with regard to all aspects and conditions of remuneration.
7 Equal Treatment Directive (76/207/EEC)	Art. 2(1) provides that '. . . the principle of equal treatment shall mean that there should be no discrimination whatsoever on grounds of sex either directly or indirectly by reference in particular to marital or family status.' The directive provides for the implementation of the principle of equal treatment for men and women as regards access to employment, vocational training and promotion and working conditions including conditions governing dismissal.

Table III

Disability legislation	Brief description
1 Disabled Persons (Employment) Act 1944 and 1958	these Acts contain the majority of the provisions which lay down the legal obligations of employers towards the disabled. The Act introduces the 3 per cent quota scheme, the register of disabled persons, the keeping of records showing whether the Act is being complied with and designated

Table III—Continued

Disability legislation	Brief description
	employment by the Secretary of State.
2 Companies (Employment of Disabled Persons) Regulations 1980	companies employing more than 250 people must contain in their Annual Directors' Report a statement outlining whatever policies have been applied in the employment, training and promotion of disabled persons.
3 Companies Act 1985	this Act makes it an offence not to produce an Annual Directors' Report of Notices (see above).
4 Chronically Sick and Disabled Persons Act 1970	the main purpose of this Act is to make provisions for physical access to public buildings and educational establishments maintaining parking facilities, sanitary conveniences and the provisions of signs.
5 Chronically Sick and Disabled Persons (Amendment) Act 1976	this amends the 1970 Act to cover places of employment.
6 Disabled Persons Act 1981	under this Act providers of premises are obliged to make appropriate provision, in accordance with standards set by the Code of Practice, for access for the disabled in buildings (BSI). The legislation also covers highways and imposes an obligation on highway authorities etc to '. . . have regard to the needs of disabled and blind persons.'
7 EEC Recommendation (OJL 86/225/43)	this states that appropriate measures to '. . . provide fair opportunities for the disabled people in the field of employment and vocational training' should be

Table III—Continued

Disability legislation	Brief description
	taken by member states. However this is not binding on member states and the British Government has not acted on it.

Race equality legislation

The Race Relations Act 1976
As noted above this Act replaced the earlier Acts of 1965 and 1968. The 1965 Act certainly did not go far enough, in that its operation was restricted to the outlawing of unfair discrimination in places of 'public resort'. The 1968 Act extended the legislation to cover employment, provision of housing and provision of services. However the mechanisms and procedures established under the Act for the enforcement of the law proved to be inadequate and excessively protracted. The 1968 Act provided that complaints should be made to the Race Relations Board, the Department of Employment or a regional Conciliation Committee. In the area of employment a number of industries had set up their own procedures for handling complaints under the Act, but where this had not happened the case was to go to the Race Relations Board to be dealt with by a conciliation officer who would set about the lengthy business of establishing all of the details of the complaints case, presenting it to the respondents and obtaining their reply. The conciliation officer would then form an opinion as to whether or not there had been unlawful discrimination. This opinion would then be communicated to the parties who would if necessary relate their cases in reply to the officer's opinion. Once all the relevant representations had been made the conciliation committee would consider the case. If the committee found that unlawful discrimination had occurred it was bound by the statute to attempt to reconcile the parties around a mutually acceptable settlement (generally damages, apologies and re-instatement) and to obtain from the employer an undertaking that such incidents would not be repeated. Failure to achieve this would result in the case going back to the Race Relations Board to decide whether or not to take action in the courts. One of the Act's main impediments was

that, being complaints-based, a large proportion of those who might have suffered discrimination inevitably failed to lodge complaints, given the possible exposure to victimization or embarrassment and an understandable reluctance to become tied up in the complex procedures just described.

It was soon generally recognized that the 1968 Act was failing to counteract racial discrimination, and that a more effective set of legislative measures would need to be enacted. The provisions of the Sex Discrimination Act 1975 provided the basic pattern which led to the enactment of the Race Relations Act 1976 and the complete repeal of the Race Relations Act 1968.

The Race Relations Act 1976 makes racial discrimination unlawful in employment, training, education, in the provision of goods and services and in the disposal and management of premises. Unlike the 1968 Act, the 1976 Act gives the aggrieved party direct access to the appropriate civil courts or tribunals in order to seek redress. The Act applies in the whole of Great Britain with the exception of Northern Ireland.

Discrimination under the 1976 Act
The definition of racial discrimination in S.1 of the Act gives rise to two kinds of discrimination commonly referred to as:

(a) direct racial discrimination

(b) indirect racial discrimination

Direct discrimination occurs where a person treats another person less favourably than he treats or would treat others *on racial grounds*. 'Racial grounds' as outlined in S.3 of the Act includes: colour, race, nationality/citizenship and ethnic or national origins.

The concept of indirect discrimination, first applied in the Sex Discrimination Act 1975, is without doubt the most significant development in the legal definitions of racial discrimination since the 1965 Act. Indirect discrimination occurs where the treatment in question is to all intents and purposes applied equally to all racial groups but emerges as having a discriminatory effect on a particular group or groups. For example, if a company advertizing a post were to state a requirement that the successful candidate should have had a British public school education, the effect would be to exclude a disproportionate section of the minority ethnic population of Britain who might otherwise be qualified for the post. In such a situation *unless the company can demonstrate that the requirement is justifiable* irrespective of colour, race, nationality or ethnic or national origins, it constitutes discrimination within the purport of the Act and as such is unlawful. It is stressed here that the burden of proof is on the alleged discriminating party to show that the cruelties and requirements are justifiable. A good deal of case law has already been built up in the courts and tribunals laying down precedents for the interpretation of central concepts such as 'less favourable', 'justifiable' and 'condition' or 'requirement' etc. (see Rubenstein M. 1988).

The Act also encompasses victimization, the definition of which is set out in S.2(1). Victimization occurs where the discriminating party treats the victimized party less favourably than he treats or would treat other persons, on the grounds that the victimized party has exercized or intends to exercize their right of complaint under the Act by bringing proceedings against the discriminating party, or by giving evidence in proceedings brought under the Act, by doing anything in connection with the proceedings being brought under the Act which affects the discriminating party or by making allegations that acts have been committed by the discriminating which contravenes the Act.

These provisions, which are unmoved in the Sex Discrimination Act 1975, were introduced in order to counteract the perceived reluctance of individuals to exercize their statutory rights of complaint for fear of retaliation or reprisal from their employers. This, as mentioned earlier, was seen to be one of the main drawbacks of the Race Relations Act 1968.

The scope of the 1976 Act
As mentioned above, the 1976 Act makes racial discrimination unlawful in employment, education and training, in the provisions of goods and services and in the disposal of premises. Let us now look at these areas in a little more detail.

Discrimination in employment
The Act makes unlawful all acts of discrimination by employers against employees in Great Britain with the exception of Northern Ireland. Employment which is wholly or mainly outside Great Britain is excluded from protection under the Act.

S.4 of the Act deals with discrimination in recruitment. It is unlawful to discriminate against job applicants in the arrangements made for deciding who should be recruited, such as in the advertizing or in the instructions given to a recruitment agency. It is not necessary to have applied for a job in order to make a complaint. It is also unlawful to discriminate in any of the terms of employment offered such as pay or holidays, and it is also unlawful deliberately to omit to offer a candidate employment – this can be done for example by deliberately omitting to consider an application.

Concerning the treatment of employees, S.4 makes it unlawful to discriminate in the terms of employment and in the provision of access to promotion, training, transfer and any other facilities or services.

Exceptions
Exceptions to the provisions outlined above include employment for the purposes of a private household, in which case discrimination is not unlawful although it remains unlawful to victimize employees. Another major exception operates in cases where it can be established that being of a particular racial group constitutes a 'genuine occupational qualification' (GOQ). S.5 of the Act cites examples where this would apply: in the sphere of dramatic performance or in the entertainment world generally, where for authenticity a performer of a particular racial group is required. Similarly in the case of restaurants where Greek, French or Chinese waiters may be necessary to provide an authentic ambience. Other examples cited refer to artistic or photographic modelling where particular racial features may be required, and there is also the example of welfare work where it can be established that the services required are best provided by people of the same racial group.

The GOQ exception does not apply where the employer already has sufficient numbers of existing employees of the racial group in question who could perform the duties required of the vacancy.

Positive action
Perhaps the most significant general exceptions to the Act's provisions against racial discriminations fall under the headings of 'positive actions'. Positive action is not to be confused with 'positive' or 'reverse' discrimination: it would be unlawful under the

Act to discriminate in favour of members of a particular racial group in order to make up for injustices or disadvantages which they have suffered historically. The Act, does, however, allow employers under S.38 to undertake positive action in favour of a particular racial group within the existing workforce under very specific circumstances.

If at any time within the preceding 12 months an employer finds that particular racial groups are markedly under-represented in any particular area of work within the establishment, it is lawful under the Act to take positive action to encourage and assist members of the racial group concerned in entering these areas of work. Such assistance might take the form of specific training facilities or the provision of opportunities to gain experience of the kind of work in question. It should be stressed that positive action is intended as a remedy for situations which lead to or perpetuate racial inequality in the workplace (positive action may also be exercized by training bodies, trade unions and employer's organizations: see S.5, 37 and 38 of the Act) and not as a means of conferring an advantage on any particular racial group.

In establishing whether or not a particular racial group is proportionally under-represented, comparison may be made either:

(a)   with the overall proportion of workers of that racial group employed within the establishment; or

(b)   with the overall proportion of that racial group within the population of the area from which the establishment could expect to recruit employees.

For a proper understanding of positive action under the Act, the following two points should be borne in mind. Firstly, that under the appropriate circumstances it may be operated in favour of the white Anglo-Saxon and Celtic ethnic majority population as well as the minority ethnic populations. Secondly, that positive actions may well not occur at the point of recruitment: to discriminate at the point of recruitment is unlawful.

The foregoing discussion of discrimination in employment has clearly been confined to the major provisions of the Act concerning employment practices in general. However, the following list of brief references will provide some indication of some of the more specific provisions of the Act affecting employment.

Section	Subject matter
7	discrimination against contract workers
10	discrimination in partnerships
11	discrimination by trade unions, employers' organizations, etc.
12	discrimination by qualifying bodies
13	discrimination by vocational training bodies
14	discrimination by employment agencies
15	discrimination by the Manpower Services Commission (MSC)

Discrimination in education
The provisions relating specifically to discrimination in education are set out in S.5, 17, 18 and 19 of the Act. The terms of the Act refer to 'educational establishments' and the corresponding 'responsible bodies' both of which are carefully defined to leave few or no loopholes. Furthermore any loopholes there may be are effectively closed by S.23 which provides that educational establishments not covered by the previous sections may find themselves subject to the Act's provisions relating to employment (see above) or the provisions relating to the provision of goods and services (see below).

Section 17 of the Act makes it unlawful for the responsible body of an educational establishment to discriminate:

(a)   in its terms of admission

(b)   by refusing or deliberately omitting to consider an application for admission

(c)   by unfair treatment with regards to access to facilities, services or other benefits

(d)   by any other unfavourable treatment or exclusion of a pupil or student.

Section 18 of the Act makes it unlawful for local education authorities in England, Scotland and Wales to discriminate in the performance of those of their statutory functions which are not covered by S.17 such as the award of discriminatory grants under the Education Act 1962.

Section 19, making specific reference to public sector education, lays down a general duty on all responsible bodies for educational establishments to ensure that all facilities and benefits provided by them for educational purposes be provided without racial discrimination.

Discrimination in the provision of goods, facilities and services
The provision of goods, facilities and services is dealt with under S.20 of the Act, which makes it unlawful for anyone engaged in providing goods and services to the public or a section of the public to discriminate by refusing or deliberately omitting to provide them, or by providing them in a manner or of a quality or on terms which discriminate unfavourably against any racial group or groups. These provisions apply irrespective of whether the goods, facilities or services are provided for payment or free of charge. However, this does not mean that the Act can be applied to transactions of a purely private nature. The scope of this section is concerned with the provision of goods, facilities and services to the public, or to a section of the public.

Discrimination in the disposal of premises
The disposal of premises is mainly dealt with by S.21 of the Act which makes it unlawful for a person who has premises at his or her disposal to discriminate either in the terms on which they are offered, in rejecting or accepting applicants for the premises or in the treatment of individual applicants in relation to housing list and the like. By the same token it is unlawful for the manager of premises, regardless of ownership or power of disposal, to discriminate in his or her treatment of the occupiers.

Other discriminatory practices
Sections 28–31 of the Act describe a range of discriminatory practices, the outlawing of which further reinforces the provisions described thus far by giving the CRE special powers to take legal proceedings, if necessary, against the perpetrators of acts which could result in indirect discrimination against a person or persons of a particular racial group. Thus there need not be a victim as such: it is sufficient that the conditions or requirements in question are potentially discriminatory for the CRE to take the appropriate steps.

Section 29 deals specifically with discriminatory advertisements and makes it unlawful to publish or place for publication an advertisement or notice which might reasonably be taken to indicate an intention to commit discriminatory acts (subject of course to the exceptions provided under the Act, such as those pursuant to positive actions, for example).

Sections 30 and 31 make it unlawful for a person who has authority over another person to instruct or otherwise cause the latter or attempt to cause the latter to carry out any act of unlawful discrimination. It is also unlawful to induce or attempt to induce an individual to commit an act of unlawful discrimination.

The role of the Commission for Racial Equality (CRE) and enforcement of the Act

The Commission for Racial Equality was set up by the Race Relations Act 1976 and does more than simply replace the former Race Relations Board, since it has far greater powers and far wider functions.

Funded by the Home Office, the CRE's budget for the 1987/88 financial year was nearly £11 million. The commission consists of 'at least eight but not more than fifteen commissioners', appointed directly by the Home Secretary, on a full-time or part-time basis and for fixed periods (not more than five years). Appointments are made on the basis of individual commissioner's relevant knowledge and experience, and they are therefore drawn from industry, commerce, the professions and education. The chair and deputy chair are also appointed by the Home Secretary. They head the regular commission and committee meetings, by which all the in-house business and proceedings are regulated.

The duties of the CRE as set out under the Act are as follows:

(i) to work towards the elimination of discrimination

(ii) to promote equality of opportunity and good relations between persons of different racial groups generally

(iii) to keep under review the working of the 1976 Act and under the appropriate circumstances to propose amendments to the Secretary of State, either at the latter's behest or on its own initiative.

The Commission is invested by the Act with a variety of powers and functions for the effective performance of the duties and objectives described above.

1 **Powers of enforcement** – the Commission's powers under S.28–31 of the Act to enforce the law against discriminatory practices have been referred to above. In addition to this the Commission is empowered under S.58 to issue non-discrimination notices where it is found on formal investigation that unlawful discrimination has occurred. The notice requires the recipient to cease in their contravention of the provisions of the Act as specified in the notice. In cases of persistent discrimination (see S.62 of the Act) the Commission may seek a court injunction against the offender.

2 **Powers of investigation** – under S.48–52 the Commission has the power to carry out formal investigations where this is in furtherance of its duties. Such investigations may either be required by the Secretary of State or they may be at the Commission's own initiative. In the former case the investigation may result in recommendations to the Secretary of State. If appropriate such recommendations may include amendments to the law. In the latter case the Commission has the power to recommend to those under investigation changes in any practices or procedures which inhibit the promotion of equal opportunities or good relations between people of different racial groups. The Commission is also empowered to require the production of oral or written evidence for the purpose of the investigation.

3 **Individual assistance** – under S.66 of the Act, the Commission may at its own discretion assist individuals who are prospective complainants. Depending on the particular circumstances, such assistance may consist of giving advice or representation.

4 As well as advising individuals the Commission may also advise employers and trade unions on general matters connected with equal opportunities.

5 S.47 of the Act provides that the Commission may publish codes of practice in order to provide guidance to those operating in the employment field as to the avoidance of discriminatory practices and the promotion of equal opportunities. As regards the legal status of codes of practice, the current Code sums up as follows:

'The Code does not impose any legal obligations

itself, nor is it an authoritative statement of the law
– that can only be provided by the courts and tribunals. If, however, its recommendations are not
observed this may result in breaches of the law where
the act of omission falls within any of the specific
prohibitions of the Act. Moreover its provisions are
admissible in evidence in any proceedings under the
Race Relations Act before an Industrial Tribunal and
if any provisions appear to the Tribunal to be relevant
to a question arising in the proceedings it must be
taken into account in determining the question.'

6   Finally, S.44 provides that the Commission may, with the
approval of the Home Office and the Treasury, provide financial assistance to any organizations which it deems to be
engaged in the promotion of equality of opportunity and good
relations between people of different racial groups.

The Commission's activities
The Commission's 1987 Annual Report (the most recent available
at the time of writing) observes that racial discrimination is still
very much a part of the modern British scene despite the many
efforts being made by the various organizations and agencies
active in the field. The Commission itself is under no illusions as
to the enormity of the task, and draws attention to the emphasis
it places on collaboration:

> 'We have enjoyed the co-operations of countless indi-
> viduals and agencies who have our goal of racial equal-
> ity, among them community relations councils, ethnic
> minority groups, voluntary organizations, churches and
> several local authorities'.

The race relations Code of Practice for employment published in
1984 is widely used by tribunals as a criterion for measuring sound
equal opportunities practices, and in a recent important decision
was cited as authority for the distribution of ethnic monitoring
data as evidence (see West Midlands Passenger Transport Executive v Singh). However, a survey of employers commissioned by
the CRE found that many employers were unaware of the Code
and that although the Code's guidelines, where implemented,

were most effective in increasing the proportion of minority ethnic employees at different levels within the workplace, for many employers equal opportunities remains an abstraction. Therefore, at least for the foreseeable future the Commission will continue to promote monitoring, targeting and positive action strategies.

In the fulfilment of its duty to keep the public informed, the CRE since its inception has produced a wide range of publications, many of which are free of charge, covering every aspect of race relations and equal opportunities. It has also been responsible for initiating many research projects as well as answering both general and specific enquiries from all sections of the public.

As mentioned earlier, one of the Commission's duties is to keep under review the working of the Race Relations Act and to make proposals to the Secretary of State where appropriate. In 1985 the Commission submitted their Review of the Race Relations Act 1976 to the Secretary of State in which various recommendations were made, aimed principally at making the law more effective against the more deep seated expressions of racial discrimination which still persist in our society. The changes proposed (these are summarized in appendix 5 of the 1985 Annual Report), if implemented, would have the effect of clarifying even further the definitions of direct and indirect discrimination, would allow for fewer exemptions from the Act, and in the area of enforcement there would be a general shift in emphasis from a persuasive and discretionary tone to a more coercive one. However, at the time of writing there has been as yet no formal response from the Government regarding the proposals.

Sex equality legislation

The major pieces of domestic legislation in the sphere of sex equality are the amended Equal Pay Act 1970 and the amended Sex Discrimination Act 1975. EEC legislation, namely the Treaty of Rome, the Directive on Equal Pay and the Equal Treatment Directive, has also had a direct impact on the area of sex equality. These will be dealt with more specifically in the section devoted to EEC legislation.

Equal Pay Act 1970

As stated earlier, the Equal Pay Act makes it unlawful to discriminate between men and women with regard to pay and other contractual terms and conditions. Other contractual terms and conditions might include, for example, holiday provisions, sick leave and redundancy payments. The provisions of the Act apply equally to both men and women. However, the far greater likelihood of women being the aggrieved parties explains the general tendency for the language of the Act to be couched primarily in terms conferring rights upon women rather than employees generally.

Section 1 of the Equal Pay Act 1970, prior to 1 January 1984, enabled women to claim equality in terms and conditions where:

(a)   they are engaged in 'like work' with men but only in cases where her work and theirs is, '. . . of the same or broadly similar nature and the difference (if any) between the things she does and the things they do are not of practical importance in relation to terms and conditions of employment . . .' (S.1(4));

(b)   they are engaged in work rated as '. . . equi-value with that of any men if, but only if, her job has been given equal value . . .' (S.1(5). In determining that the jobs are of equal value a proper job evaluation study would need to have been carried out for the specific purpose.

Since 1 January 1984 a third avenue has been opened up whereby women may pursue claims to equal pay. Proceedings brought against the British Government by the European Commission in order to bring it in line with the Equal Pay Directive (75/117/EEC), gave rise to the Equal Pay (Amendment) Regulations 1983, now encapsulated within S.1(2)(c) of the Equal Pay Act, which makes it possible for women to be engaged in work of 'equal value' to that of a man in terms of such criteria as effort, skill and decision making, to bring a claim for equal pay. There is no requirement that the job is the same or broadly similar as in S.1(4), and neither is a job evaluation required as in S.1(5).

Comparison under the Act

The Equal Pay Act does not allow comparisons with persons of the same sex in pursuance of a claim for equal pay. A woman may compare herself with a man (and a man only with a woman), who must be employed by the same or an associated employer. For these purposes an associated employer is one which comes under the direct or indirect control of the other or where both companies come under the control of a third company.

Like work – S.1(4)

In determining whether or not a woman is engaged in like work with men, it must be established first, whether or not the work is the same or of a broadly similar nature. Where the work is the same, the matter is straightforward. On the other hand, where the work is broadly similar it must be determined whether or not the differences amount to factors of practical importance in relation to the terms and conditions of employment as intended by S.1(4) of the Act. The relevant case law establishes that the Industrial Tribunal has to make a broad judgment on the basis of its experience and of its knowledge of the real world. Therefore, trifling distinctions which in the real world could not be expected to be reflected in the contractual terms of employment would be disregarded. Case law also establishes that it is not sufficient merely that differences in contractual terms exist: they must also amount to some practical importance. Therefore, where additional contractual duties appear in the man's job which in practical terms are rarely or only occasionally performed, they will not be held to be of practical importance within the meaning of S.1(4). The Tribunal may also use as a guide whether or not the differences would be such as to place the jobs in different categories or grades in a job evaluation study.

Equivalent work S.1(5)

Work which is rated as equi-value signifies that a valid job evaluation study, organized under various headings such as skill, effort and decision-making, has found the jobs in question to be equivalent. There is no obligation under the Act for an employer to undertake such a study, but where it has done so its findings may be used as the basis for a claim. Where the evaluation shows the jobs not to be equivalent the claimant clearly will not be able to base her case upon it. However, the claimant can show whether the study was carried out in a discriminatory manner or whether there is discrimination in evaluating between men and women, when her claim may still succeed providing her job would have been rated as equivalent if not for the discrimination. The following example may help to clarify the principle:

A job evaluation study has been carried out in an industrial cleaning company which employs both men and women. Both men and women are required to be engaged in 'heavy duty' cleaning work. However, the study allocates a certain weighting to men's heavy duty work while allocating a lesser weighting to women's heavy duty work. In such circumstances a woman could still bring her claim by showing that if not for the discrimination in the weighting, her job would have been valued as equivalent.

Equal value
As indicated above, since 1 January 1984 it has been possible for a woman to bring an equal pay claim for work of equal value without needing to demonstrate that the jobs are broadly similar and without reliance on a valid job evaluation study. In fact, as in the case of equivalent work, even where a job evaluation study has been carried out and has found the jobs to be unequal, the claimant may still bring her claim if she can show grounds for suspecting discrimination within the study.

A job evaluation could be shown to have discriminated indirectly against women where a high weighting is attached to an element which forms a significant part of the job carried out by men but only a minimal part in the work done by women, i.e. a study which gives a high weighting to heavy manual labour while giving a relative low weighting to light machining work is on the face of it discriminatory.

Defence to equal pay claims
Section 1(3) of the Equal Pay Act provides as follows:

> 'An equality clause shall not operate in relation to a variation between the woman's contract and the man's contract if the employer proves that the variation is genuinely due to a material factor which is not the defence of sex . . .'

Whether a claim is being made on the basis that the work is the same or broadly similar or whether the claim is based on equal value, the burden of proof is on the employer to show that there are material factors within the purport of the Act which justify the difference in treatment. The case law has established that material factors include qualifications, length of service and experience. Where the claim is being brought for equal value (as opposed to 'like work' and 'equivalent work') the possibilities for justification are made broader and may extend outside the factors specific to the individual's personal qualities. For example, case law has established that market forces are a relevant material factor: if for example all else (i.e. effort, skill and decision making) is equal between a light machinist and an HGV driver, it is open to the employer to justify the latter's higher pay by showing that it would be impossible to recruit drivers otherwise. Clearly, there are many examples and it is important to stress that each case is decided upon its own merits.

The Sex Discrimination Act 1975

The Sex Discrimination Act 1975 (SDA) makes sex discrimination unlawful in employment, training, education, in the provision of goods and services and in the disposal and management of premises. The Act applies to the whole of Great Britain with the exception of Northern Ireland.

As stated earlier the provision of the SDA applies equally to discrimination against either sex, but given the greater likelihood of women being subjected to unequal treatment on grounds of sex, they are inevitably the main beneficiaries in practice.

Discrimination under the Act

As mentioned above in the section dealing with race legislation, the SDA to a very significant degree formed the basic blueprint on which the RRA 1976 was modelled and, like the RRA, S.1 of the SDA establishes two kinds of discrimination:

(a) direct sex discrimination

(b) indirect sex discrimination

Direct discrimination occurs where on grounds of her sex a woman is treated less favourably than a man.

Indirect discrimination is defined in S.1(1)(b) of the Act:

'A person discriminates against a woman where:
. . . he applies to her a requirement or condition which applies or would apply equally to a man but

(i) which is such that the proportion of women who can comply with it is considerably smaller than the proportion of men who can comply with it, and

(ii) which he cannot show to be justifiable irrespective of the sex of the person to whom it is applied, and

(iii) which is to her detriment because she cannot comply with it.'

For example, if an employer advertising a post for a retail skills instructor were to include a requirement that the successful candidates should be at least six feet tall, it would have the effect of excluding a disproportionate section of the female population. The fact that some women could comply with the condition or that a significant proportion of the male population would also be excluded is neither here nor there: the fact remains that the proportion of women able to comply with it is considerably smaller than the proportion of men able to comply with it. It is highly unlikely that the employer would be able to justify such a condition under paragraph (ii) above and the conditions in paragraph (iii) that it should be to a woman's detriment that she cannot comply with it would most certainly be satisfied. Therefore it is clear that that requirement is indirectly discriminatory within the meaning of the Act.

Discrimination under the SDA also covers discrimination against married persons. Section 3(1) of the Act provides:

'A person discriminates against a married person of either sex in any circumstances relevant for the purposes of Part II if –

(a) on the grounds of his or her marital status he treats that person less favourably than he treats or would treat an unmarried person of the same sex, or

    (b)   he applies to that person a requirement or condition which he applies or would apply equally to an unmarried person but –

        (i)   which is such that the proportion of married persons who can comply with it is considerably smaller than the proportion of unmarried persons of the same sex who can comply with it, and

        (ii)   which he cannot show to be justifiable irrespective of the marital status of the person to whom it is applied, and

        (iii)   which is to that person's detriment because he cannot comply with it.'

The provisions are clearly a mirror image of those relating to direct and indirect sex discrimination described previously. However, it is important to be aware that the provisions relating to discrimination against married persons in S.3(1) relate *exclusively* to Part II of the Act which is concerned with discrimination in the area of employment.

As with the Race Relations Act 1976, the SDA also makes provision for cases of victimization, set out in S.4(1) of the Act. Victimization arises where the discriminator treats the victimized party (who may be of either sex) less favourably than he treats, or would treat, other persons, on the grounds that the victimized party has exercized or intends to exercize (or is suspected of having done so or intending to do so) their rights under the SDA or the Equal Pay Act 1970 by doing any of the following:

(a)   bringing proceedings against the discriminator under either Act

(b)   giving evidence or information in proceedings brought under either Act

(c)   doing anything in connection with proceedings being brought under either Act which affects the discriminator

(d)   making allegations that actions have been committed by the discriminator which would contravene the SDA or provide grounds for a claim under the EPA. In this case however, it does not constitute victimization under the Act if the allegation is fake and is not made in good faith.

Discrimination in employment
The Act makes unlawful all acts of discrimination by employers against their employees in Great Britain. Employment which is wholly or mainly outside Great Britain (with certain exceptions relating to aircraft and shipping) is excluded from protection under the Act.

S.6 of the 1975 Act deals with discrimination in recruitment and treatment of employees in the same way as the RRA 1976 described earlier, with the additional provision (S.8) that if an employer discriminates in relation to terms offered such as pay or holidays when recruiting employees in such a manner as to be in breach of the EPA 1970, this would automatically become unlawful under the SDA. With regard to the treatment of current employees in relation to retirement provisions, important additions are introduced by the Sex Discrimination Act 1986 (SDA 1986). The SDA 1986 provides that from 7 November 1987 employers cannot set different compulsory retirement ages for men and women in comparable positions. They are further prohibited from refusing opportunities for training, promotion or transfer on the basis of retirement.

Exceptions – private household and small firms
Prior to 7 February 1987, employment in private households and small firms (ie those not employing more than five people) was exempt from the requirements set out in S.6 of the SDA 1975 which make it unlawful for employers to discriminate in recruitment or against existing employees. However, since that date the SDA 1986 has come into force introducing various amendments aimed at bringing the law in line with the Equal Treatment Directive (76/207(EEC)). As a result, this exception has been repealed therefore it is no longer lawful for firms, no matter how small, to discriminate on grounds of sex or marriage. In the case of private households the same would apply except that the SDA 1986 introduces a new Genuine Occupational Qualification which under certain conditions permits sex discrimination but not discrimination on grounds of marriage.

Pregnancy
S.2 of the SDA 1975 allows employers to discriminate in favour of women in relation to pregnancy and childbirth. Therefore employers may for example institute special treatment in terms of maternity leave.

Genuine Occupational Qualifications (GOQ)
The exception of GOQ applies to sex discrimination only and cannot be used to justify discrimination on grounds of marriage, or victimization. GOQ is covered by S.7 of the SDA 1975, which outlines a range of instances in which a person's sex may be regarded as a GOQ. These are summarized below:

(a) where it is essential to the job for physiological purposes (apart from physical strength) or for purposes of authenticity, eg modelling or acting

(b) where requirements of decency or privacy dictate that the job holder should be of the same sex as the person with whom they will be coming into contact in the course of his/her work, eg changing-room attendant. As indicated above, the SDA 1986 has extended this general principle to employment in private households so that reasonable objection to someone of the opposite sex sharing the intimacy of one's home or having a certain degree of physical contact is justifiable under the SDA. An example of such a post might be a nurse

(c) where there is a lack of separate sleeping or sanitary facilities for each sex and where the nature or location of the establishment would make it impracticable for the job holder to live elsewhere. This does not apply however where the employers could reasonably be expected to provide separate facilities

(d) where the job is in an establishment or part of an establishment which provides special care, supervision or attention for one sex only, eg some jobs in a women's hospital

(e) where the job involves the provision of personal services promoting welfare, education or similar services and those services are best provided by job holders of one particular sex, eg a female welfare worker may be more effective in certain cases involving women

(f)   where the job holder has to be a man because of legal restrictions regulating the employment of women, eg factories legislation imposes various restrictions regarding the hours, location, conditions etc in which women may be employed. (It should be noted here that legislation currently going through Parliament is seeking to repeal this particular provision – see discussion of the Employment Bill below)

(g)   where the country in which a part of the job is to be performed has laws or customs which require certain jobs to be done by men only or women only, eg in some countries women may not drive

(h)   where the job is one of two to be held by a married couple.

The GOQ exception does not apply where the employer has sufficient existing employees who could perform the duties required without undue inconvenience.

Retirement
S.6 SDA 1975 in combination with S.2 SDA 1986 provides that it is not unlawful for an employer to discriminate in the provisions he makes in relation to death or retirement. However, from 7 November 1987 employers can no longer set different compulsory retirement ages for men and women in comparable positions.

Positive action
It is certainly worth repeating here what was said earlier in relation to positive action under the Race Relations Act 1976. Positive action is not to be confused with positive or 'reverse' discrimination: it is unlawful under the SDA to discriminate in favour of women in order to make up for historical injustices or disadvantages. However, the Act does permit employers under S.48 to institute positive action measures.

   If at any time within the previous 12 months an employer finds that particular work is being done exclusively by one sex, or that the number of persons of one sex doing the work is small compared to the number of persons of the other sex, it is lawful under the Act for the employer to take positive action to encourage and assist the minority sex. Assistance may take the form of special access to training and encouragement to take up opportunities to do the work in question. Two points need to be borne in mind regarding the working of the positive action provisions. Firstly, that where appropriate it may be operated in favour of men as well as women. Secondly, that it is unlawful to discriminate at the point of recruitment. Positive action aims at eradicating from the workplace practices and circumstances which tend to perpetuate discrimination between the sexes. In this regard it is relevant to note that positive action may also be exercized by trade unions and employers' organizations.

Acts performed under statutory authority of prior legislation
S.51 SDA 1975 provides a general exception for acts which are performed in order to comply with legislation passed prior to the SDA 1975. This section has significant implications for women, particularly with regard to much of the protective legislation passed prior to the SDA placing various restrictions on women's working conditions. (It should be noted here that the European Commission has expressed the opinion that S.51 is in conflict with the Equal Treatment Directive and that the Government has accepted this view – the matter is discussed in more detail in chapter 7.)

The legislation described above deals only with the major provisions relating to discrimination in employment. The list below provides a brief guide to other areas of the employment field.

SDA section	Subject matter
9	discrimination against contract workers
11	discrimination against partners. (This section has been amended by the SDA 1986 to make it applicable to firms of all sizes and not just those of six or more partners)
12	discrimination by trade unions, employers organizations, etc.
13	discrimination by qualifying bodies
14	discrimination by vocational training bodies
15	discrimination by employment agencies
16	discrimination by the MSC

Discrimination in education

As in the case of the Race Relations Act 1976, the SDA's provisions relating to discrimination in education make reference to 'educational establishments' and their corresponding 'responsible bodies' both of which are carefully defined in S.22 of the Act, which states that it is unlawful for the responsible body or an educational establishment to discriminate:

(a)   in its terms of admission

(b)   by refusing or deliberately omitting to accept an application for admission

(c)   in the way it provides access to facilities, services or other benefits

(d)   by treating a student unfavourably or excluding him or her.

S.23 SDA makes it unlawful for education authorities in England, Wales and Scotland to discriminate in the performance of their duties under the Education Acts such as in awarding discretionary grants and the provision of certain other educational facilities.

   S.25 of the Act establishes a general duty on responsible bodies in the field of public sector education to ensure that educational facilities and other benefits provided by them for educational purposes are provided without sex discrimination. This general duty is enforceable by the Secretary of State for Education and Science.

   The Act provides for certain exemptions from the requirements against discrimination:

(i)   S.26 exempts single-sex establishments and school boarding accommodation

(ii)   S.27 provides that single-sex establishments which wish to become co-educational over a period of time may apply for a transitional exemption order so that a boys' school for example could during the period of transition lawfully restrict the admission of boys in favour of girls

(iii)   S.28 provides exemption for further education courses in physical training

(iv) SS.78 and 79 allow education charities to fulfil charitable provisions where beneficiaries are of one sex only.

Discrimination in the provision of goods and services

S.29 of the SDA 1975 contains the provisions relating to the provision of goods and services. In general the approach is an exact reflection of that taken by S.20 Race Relations Act 1976 described in the previous section. In other words, it is unlawful for anyone engaged in providing goods and services to the public to discriminate by refusing or deliberately omitting to provide them or by offering them in a way or of a quality which is discriminatory. Examples of facilities and services cited by the SDA are:

(a) access to and use of any place which members of the public are permitted to enter

(b) accommodation in a hotel, boarding-house etc

(c) banking, insurance and finance facilities

(d) facilities for education, instruction or training

(e) facilities for entertainment, recreation or refreshment

(f) facilities for transport or travel

(g) the services of any professional, trade or public authority.

As in the RRA 1976, where provisions apply only where the discrimination is by persons concerned with the provision of goods, facilities and services to the public, or a section of the public. It does not apply to transactions of a purely private nature. In addition, a person who provides goods, facilities and services which are designed for use by one sex is not required to provide the equivalent items for the other sex. Specific exceptions to the provisions of S.29 SDA are:

(a) facilities provided by establishments for persons requiring special care, supervision or attention

(b) facilities etc. provided at places used for religious purposes

(c) facilities etc. provided in situations which demand restriction of facilities to one sex only for the preservation of privacy and decency

(d)   facilities etc. provided under the constitution, organization or administration of a political party.

There are two more exceptions given below which relate specifically to premises.

Discrimination in the disposal of premises
This is covered by S.30 SDA 1975 and once more is stated in the same terms as the RRA 1976, making it unlawful for a person with premises at their disposal to discriminate either in the terms at which they are offered or in rejecting or accepting applicants for the premises or in the treatment of application in relation to housing lists etc. There are however, the following exceptions (these also apply to the provisions of goods, facilities and services under S.29):

(a)   where the premises are small it is not unlawful to discriminate when the person who has responsibility for the premises is a near relative, lives on the premises and shares the accommodation with other occupiers who are not members of his household

(b)   non-profit making establishments not set up by statute may lawfully restrict their membership and other facilities and benefits to one sex only.

Other discriminatory practices
SS.37–42 SDA 1975 describe various practices which, while not amounting to unlawful discrimination under any of the provisions of the Act covered so far, would result in or might result in unlawful indirect discrimination. The Act confers upon the Equal Opportunities Commission (as in the case of the CRE) special powers to bring legal proceedings in cases of contravention of these provisions. Therefore, as under the sister provisions of the RRA 1976, there need be no victim as such. It is required only that the conduct in question is potentially discriminatory.

S.38 deals specifically with discriminatory advertisements in practically identical terms to S.29 of the RRA 1976 (see above). S.39 makes it unlawful for a person who has authority over another person to instruct that person to commit an act of unlawful discrimination. S.40 makes it unlawful to bring pressure to bear on another person to commit an act of unlawful discrimination. Such pressure may take the form of inducements or threats. S.42 covers the aiding of unlawful discrimination. Anyone who knowingly acts or assists in an act defined by the SDA as unlawful will be treated as though he had committed the act himself. However, the person will not be treated as having aided the act where he placed reasonable reliance on a statement by the other person that the act in question was subject to exemption from the provision of the SDA.

The role of the Equal Opportunities Commission and enforcement of the Act

The EOC's powers of enforcement in relation to the SDA 1975 and EPA 1970 are identical to those exercised by the CRE in relation to the RRA 1976, in terms of being able to issue non-discrimination notices, to bring legal proceedings in respect of persistent discrimination and discriminatory practices, and in being able to offer assistance to the individual complaints in appropriate circumstances. The EOC's powers of investigation provided under SS.57–60 are also to all intents and purposes identical to those of the CRE. It is also funded by the Home Office; its 1988/89 budget was £3.8 million and its commissioners are appointed in the same way as those for the CRE. Like the CRE, the EOC is given the power to publish codes of practice (S.56 SDA 1975) which may contain guidance for the elimination of discrimination in the field of employment and/or the promotion of equality of opportunity in employment between men and women. The Act provides that a code of practice issued by the EOC is admissible in evidence in tribunal proceedings, which will take any of its relevant provisions into account.

The commission's activities

In line with its duty to work towards the elimination of discrimination and so promote equality of opportunity between men and women, the EOC has produced a wide range of publications providing easy access to guidance and information on all practical aspects of legislation and good practice in the field of sex equality, including the codes of practice referred to above.

In terms of their duty to keep under review the working of the SDA and EPA, the EOC has been particularly active of late. On the basis of replies to their consultative document *Legislating for*

Change? issued in 1986, the Commission was able to publish in 1988 formal proposals for amending the SDA and EPA in their document, *Equal Treatment for Men and Women – strengthening the Acts.* The review proposes a new Act which would rationalize the confusion and complexities presently being caused by the need to reconcile the various sources of European and domestic sex discrimination law. The new Act would be called the Equal Treatment Act and would incorporate the SDA 1975 and the EPA 1970 and would take into account the standards and provisions required by European law. The review sets out a comprehensive range of recommendations and amendments to existing legislation, based on the EOC's conviction that although the basic approach of the SDA and EPA is sound, there remains much inequality and certain shortcomings.

The overall stance of the new comprehensive Act would build on the foundations established by current legislation by establishing 'a positive atmosphere for future development'. It would work on the principle that women have a positive right to equal treatment as opposed to the negatively expressed right not to be discriminated against. This is a brief summary of the main proposals:

(i)   in cases of indirect discrimination a strict test of justifiability be applied so that an employer would need to show that the requirement in question is justified on objective economic grounds and would be necessary to the achievement of the aims of the business. Such an adjustment would be in line with European Court of Justice law (Bilka v Weber)

(ii)   a change in the burden of proof so that once the applicant proves less favourable treatment in circumstances consistent with grounds of sex or victimization, a presumption of discrimination should arise which would require the respondent to prove that there were grounds other than sex or victimization to justify the treatment

(iii)   due to the uncertainty and complexity of the law relating to questions of death and retirement, the provisions of the SDA 1975 and the EPA 1970 which create exceptions from the general provisions of the Acts (S.6(4) and S.6(1A)(b) respectively) should be repealed at the earliest opportunity

(iv)   the EOC's own powers of investigation should be reinforced so that the Commission can investigate a named person or organization for any purpose connected with the fulfilment of its duties. Also that the EOC should be granted a general power to bring legal proceedings against any person it suspects of unlawful discrimination

(v) a statutory duty should be imposed on all bodies to carry out a service or undertaking of a public nature to work towards the elimination of discrimination and to promote equality of opportunity.

These are just some of the more immediately striking recommendations made in the review of the legislation.

The Employment Bill

At the time of writing the Government's Employment Bill which is going through Parliament is likely to introduce fundamental changes in equal opportunities law as it affects the employment of women. In the consultative document put before the Government in December 1987, the view was expressed that a great deal of the existing protective legislation requiring different treatment for men and women would nowadays be seen as 'restricting the employment opportunities of women rather than protecting them'. Hence the Bill sets out provisions which, if passed into law in their current form, will restrict significantly the range of circumstances in which sex discrimination will be permitted in order to protect women. The main importance of the key clauses is summarized below:

Clause 2 – this clause gives the Secretary of State powers to make an Order amending or repealing existing discriminatory legislation in the field of employment and vocational training passed prior to the Bill, including those which the Bill itself for the time being deems lawful.

Clause 3 – this clause is of major significance with regard to equal opportunities for women in employment. It replaces S.51 SDA 1975 with a new S.51 and S.51A, and it repeals S.7(2)(f) which provides a GOQ exception where the job needs to be held by a man because of restrictions imposed by the laws regulating the employment of women. The new S.51 restricts permitted discrimination in employment and vocational training to situations where it is necessary to comply with statutory requirements enacted prior to the SDA 1975, where the purpose is the protection of women *in relation to pregnancy or maternity or other circumstances involving risks specific to women.*

Clause 12 – this clause provides the other major change introduced by the Bill, by giving women the right to receive statutory redundancy payments up to the age of 65 to put them on the same footing as men.

Clause 16 – this clause allows a pre-hearing review to be carried out before an industrial tribunal, and if appropriate to order the claimant to pay £150 deposit before proceeding to a full tribunal. This is meant to deter claimants who have no chance of success or who are pursuing a frivolous case.

A further instance of the Commission's recent activity relates specifically to equal pay. The Commission has this year issued a consultative document entitled *Equal Pay . . . Making it Work* recommending that the present equal pay law should be made simpler, quicker and cheaper to administer. The document states that present legislation:

> 'serves individuals badly, groups of workers hardly at all and does little to encourage the voluntary process'.

The document is primarily concerned with assisting women in segregated jobs who suffer most from discriminatory pay, by making the law accessible to them. With this objective in mind the Commission suggests various possible changes which would:

(a) enhance the EPA's ability to cater for discrimination against groups of workers

(b) improve procedures for dealing with individual complaints

(c) amend certain provisions of the substantive law established by the Act.

Copies of this document have been sent to interested parties and relevant sectors of the industry, unions and professions for comments. These comments will form part of the Government's consultative process on the Bill.

Disability legislation

Legislation aimed at people with disabilities in Britain has a far longer history than the 'equal opportunities' legislation described so far, which aims specifically at race and sex equality.

Clearly in all societies and at all times disabled people have always existed. Prior to this century it has generally been the lot of voluntary charity organizations, and self-help, to achieve any meaningful progress towards improving the welfare of the disabled population. By the early decades of this century this state of affairs had already changed. After the First World War and the subsequent focus on those who had suffered injuries, pressure groups demanding specific provisions became more vociferous and insistent, giving rise to the partnership which still operates today between the voluntary and the statutory sectors. By the end of the Second World War, preoccupation with the rehabilitation of the injured was further intensified, eventually prompting the passage of major pieces of legislation which made provisions for those disabled people classified as being able to participate in the labour market. These were the Disabled Persons (Employment) Acts of 1944 and 1958, which will be examined in more detail below along with other more recent legislation extending beyond the employment field into other key areas such as access, housing and education.

The Disabled Persons (Employment) Acts 1944 and 1958

These Acts contain the majority of the legislation covering the legal obligations of employers towards the disabled. Perhaps the best known of this is the three per cent quota scheme which has been and continues to be the subject of much debate. The Acts also introduced the register of disabled persons, the obligation of keeping records to determine whether or not the Acts are being complied with, and certain types of 'designated employment' designated by the Secretary of State for the registered disabled. In fact it is the 1944 Act which contains these provisions and which will be examined in greater detail below. The 1958 Act introduces certain amendments regarding the minimum age for registration under the Act and the power of local authorities to provide sheltered employment such as sheltered workshops and placement schemes.

The 1944 Act covers disability, courses for vocational training and rehabilitation, obtaining employment or entering self-employment for the registered disabled, and general application and enforcement of the provisions.

Definition of disability
Section 1 of the Act defines disability as follows:

> '. . . "disabled persons" means a person who, on account of injury, disease or congenital deformity is substantially handicapped in obtaining or in keeping employment or in undertaking work on his own account, of a kind which apart from that injury, disease or deformity would be suited to his age, experience and qualifications.'

Training and rehabilitation
Section 2 contains provisions which allow the appropriate government departments to arrange training courses for young disabled people beyond the compulsory school leaving age.

Sections 3–5 make provision for the establishment of Industrial Rehabilitation Units now run by the Training Agency and renamed Employment Rehabilitation Centres. The facilities provided by the Act include training courses and the necessary financial assistance for people attending them.

Disabled persons register
Sections 6–8 establish the disabled persons register and set out the conditions for registration. Registration may last from one to ten years, after which time it may be renewed provided the necessary requirements are met. On registration the disabled person is issued with a 'green card' which gives access to certain facilities such as employment under the quota scheme, designated employment, employment in sheltered workshops, assistance with travel expenses to and from work and access to aids and adaptations via the Training Agency. Registration under the Act is entirely voluntary.

Standard and special quotas

Sections 9, 10 and 11 of the Act are concerned with the establishment of a freed quota of disabled persons which employers are required to recruit. Employers of 20 or more workers are under a duty to provide employment for registered disabled people up to a certain proportion of their entire workforce. The standard percentage currently stands at three per cent. It is an offence not to employ a suitable disabled person if the employer in question has not met the standard quota of three per cent, the penalty being a fine not exceeding £100, or imprisonment for a term not exceeding three months, or both. It is open to employers to apply for a permit to employ non-registered disabled persons where it is ascertained that the register does not contain a suitable disabled person.

The Act also makes provision for the application of a 'special percentage' as opposed to the standard three per cent. However, the only special case so far applies to employment as a master or member of the crew of a British ship where the quota is 0.1%.

It is not an offence in itself to be below quota but it is an offence to recruit non-registered disabled persons while below quota without a prior permit. It is also an offence to dismiss a registered disabled employee without reasonable cause, where the employer is below the quota or where this would cause the employer to fall below the quota. Disputes in such cases may be brought before the district Committee for Employment of Disabled People (CEDP).

Section 12 of the Act gives the government, through the appropriate minister, the power to designate certain categories of employment as automatically amenable to disabled people, and as such they do not count towards the three per cent quota. So far the occupations designated are car park attendants and lift attendants.

Disability records

Section 14 of the Act states that all those employers subject to the quota scheme should keep records which show to what extent they are in compliance with the requirements of the Act. These records may be subject to inspection by the Department of Employment and must be preserved for a period of two years.

Seriously disabled persons
Section 15 of the Act gives the appropriate minister the power to provide financial support for the setting up of companies which provide sheltered employment for individuals who are so severely disabled as to have very little likelihood of finding ordinary employment or of becoming self-employed. One example of such a company is Remploy.

The effectiveness of the quota scheme
There can be little doubt that the original objectives of enabling disabled people to obtain and retain meaningful employment remain unfulfilled by the quota scheme. The National Audit Office reporting in 1987 found that between 1965 and 1986 the proportion of the employers meeting the quota had fallen from 53 to 27 per cent. Over the same period, the proportion of employers with permits of exemption had risen from 28 to 56 per cent. Between 1950 and 1986 the number of disabled persons registering had fallen from 936,000 to 389,000, representing one per cent of the labour force. This figure quite clearly does not provide an accurate indication of the numbers of disabled people.

The National Audit Office concludes in their report that not only is the quota scheme costly to administer, but that it is also:

> '. . . ineffective, unenforceable and incapable of achieving its aim of getting employers to recruit three per cent of their workforce from the disabled adult workforce'.

The IPM, in its comments to the Secretary of State on the review of the quota scheme compiled by the MSC (1981), draws attention to the negativity of the emphasis placed on disability itself:

> '(the quota scheme) . . . has had the dual effect of pressuring employers to ensure their disabled employees register, (a retrogressive step as it emphasizes the very thing that should not be emphasized, that is, the person's disability) . . . The scheme is also counter productive concentrating, as it does, on a person's disabilities rather than his or her abilities.'

The IPM makes the following recommendations for a more positive approach:

(a) a requirement on employers to designate certain jobs for certain people with disabilities

(b) grants to help provide suitable facilities for the disabled

(c) encouragement for employers to place orders with sheltered workshops

(d) a reduced employers' national insurance repayment for disabled employees, as defined.

Finally it is difficult to avoid the conclusions of the IPM's National Committee – Pay and Employment Conditions submitted to the MSC in 1987:

> 'We have long pressed for the abolition of the quota scheme which by any definition has outlived its usefulness. Almost irrespective of the research being carried out in the quota . . . the quota is irrelevant. When the registered disabled amount to less than one per cent of the total workforce, a quota of three per cent only serves to bring the law into disrepute'.

The Companies (Directors' Report) (Employment of Disabled Persons) Regulations 1980

These regulations, which have now been incorporated into the Companies Act 1985 (S. 235 part III Schedule 7), provide that companies employing on average over 250 people must contain in their Annual Directors' Report a policy statement outlining whatever measures have been applied regarding the recruitment, training and promotion of disabled persons, including the non-registered disabled. The Act makes it an offence not to comply with these requirements. However, public sector employers are exempt, although they are advised by the Department of Trade and Industry to apply the rules.

The Chronically Sick and Disabled Persons Act 1970

The main purpose of this highly significant piece of legislation is to make provision for physical access to public buildings, educational establishments, parking facilities and the provision of signs. The Chronically Sick and Disabled Persons (Amendment) Act 1976 extends the 1970 Act to cover access to places of employment.

Section 1 of the Act places a duty on all local authorities to inform themselves of the number of persons in their area who need particular services and to take steps to meet these needs. This duty includes finding out the needs of the disabled in their area and assessing how they could benefit from any support provided by the authority. This has led to significant efforts and improvements in the services provided for disabled people in many local authority areas.

Section 2 of the Act refers to 'practical assistance' and includes such support as home helps, meals, aids and adaptations and recreational facilities. It also includes help with travel.

Section 3 provides that local authorities, when constructing new housing, must include in their proposals any measures they intend to take for the disabled. They must also '. . . have regard to the special needs of chronically sick or disabled persons'.

Sections 20 and 21 deal with the use of the public highways by the disabled and introduces the 'Orange Badge Scheme' which are issued by local authorities '. . . for motor vehicles driven by or used for the carriage of disabled persons.'

Section 22 provides that the Secretary of State presents annually a report to Parliament on the:

> '. . . research and development work carried out by or on behalf of any Minister of the Crown in relation to equipment that might increase the range of activities and independence or well-being of disabled persons, and in particular such equipment that might improve the indoor and outdoor mobility of such persons.'

The Disabled Persons Act 1981

Under this Act, providers of premises are obliged to make appropriate provision in accordance with standards set by the Code of Practice for Access for the Disabled in Buildings (BSI). The Act also makes further provisions regarding public highways, imposing a duty on highway authorities and others carrying out works on highways to have regard to the needs of disabled and blind persons.

It also requires the Secretary of State to report to Parliament proposals for improving or facilitating access to public buildings and buildings used by the public.

Other legislation
Clearly there are many other pieces of general legislation which affect people with disabilities and which apply equally to people without disabilities, and as such are seen as outside of the scope of the present chapter (eg the Factories Acts, the Health and Safety at Work Act 1974 and the Employment Protection Act 1975). There are also many other pieces of legislation which do have specific application to the disabled but insufficient direct bearing on matters of equal opportunities to merit specific attention in this chapter.

As far as European legislation is concerned, there is only a general recommendation (OJL 86/225/43) which states that appropriate measures to '. . . provide fair opportunities for the disabled people in the field of employment and vocational training' should be taken by member states. However, EEC recommendations are not binding on member states and the British government has not so far acted upon it.

EEC law and the member states

EEC law is an independent legal system which is common to all member states. It overrides national law, and can impose binding duties on governments and individuals. It consists of the Treaty of Rome and 'secondary legislation' – directives, regulations and recommendations – prepared by the European Commission and approved by the Council of Ministers. The law is interpreted by the European Court of Justice.

Two basic principles govern the relationship between EEC and member states:

1   the supremacy of EEC law cannot be overriden by domestic law. If there is a conflict between the two, EEC law takes precedence. In theory this is contrary to the UK doctrine of

Parliamentary Sovereignty which states the need for Parliament to ratify each piece of legislation. This was overcome by the European Communities Act 1972 which ratifies any present or future EEC legislation.

2 'direct effect' – in some provisions of EEC law an individual in a member state pursuing the right of 'direct effect' can take action to their domestic courts based on EEC law.

Individuals do not have direct access to the European Court: cases are referred by the European Commission under infringement proceedings or by national courts or tribunals.

Because of the overriding nature of EEC law, member states are meant to ensure that the objectives of directives are achieved. If they are not, the Commission may instigate infringement proceedings against the state. The UK has been taken to the European Court of Justice on two occasions by the Commission for infringement of the Equal Pay Directive and the Equal Treatment Directive.

Individuals who consider their rights, as defined by EEC law, have been infringed, must first bring an action in a national court or tribunal. If that court feels it needs EEC interpretation of the law, or if it is the final court of appeal, it will request the European Court of Justice to give a ruling.

EEC legislation

This section outlines the main direction of EEC legislation in each area. These directives have not necessarily been fully implemented in the UK. For more detailed interpretation, the relative directives should be consulted. These directives are exclusively applied to sex discrimination. In the UK, because of the workforce and the legislative background, sex legislation and race discrimination legislation have been developed in parallel. There is no reason at this stage to anticipate that this will change.

EEC Treaty – Article 189
In order to carry out their task the Council and the Commission shall, in accordance with the provisions of this Treaty, make regulations, issue directives, take decisions, make recommendations or deliver opinions.

A regulation shall have a general application. It shall be binding in its entirety and directly applicable in all member states.

A directive shall be binding, as to the result to be achieved, upon each member state to which it is addressed, but shall leave to the national authorities the choice of form and methods.

A decision shall be binding in its entirety upon those to whom it is addressed.

Recommendations and opinions shall have no binding force.

Equal Treatment Directive – Article 6

Member states shall introduce into their national legal systems such measures as are necessary to enable all persons who consider themselves wronged by failure to apply to them the principle of equal treatment within the meaning of Articles 3, 4 and 5 to pursue their claims by judicial process after possible resource to other competent authorities.

Equal Treatment Directive – Article 1

1   the purpose of this Directive is to put into effect in the member states the principle of equal treatment for men and women as regards access to employment, including promotion, and to vocational training, and as regards working conditions and, on the conditions referred to in paragraph 2, social security. This principle is hereinafter referred to as 'the principle of equal treatment'.

2   with a view to ensuring the progressive implementation of the principle of equal treatment in matters of social security, the Council, acting on a proposal from the Commission will adopt provisions defining its substance, its scope and the arrangements for its application.

Equal Treatment Directive – Article 5

1   application of the principle of equal treatment with regard to working conditions, including the conditions governing dismissal, means that men and women shall be guaranteed the same conditions without discrimination on grounds of sex.

Social Security Directive – Article 7

1   this directive shall be without prejudice to the right of member states to exclude from its scope:

(a) the determination of pensionable age for the purposes of granting old-age and retirement pensions and the possible consequences thereof for other benefits

(b) advantages in respect of old-age pension schemes granted to persons who have brought up children; the acquisition of benefit entitlements following periods of interruption of employment due to the bringing up of children

(c) the granting of old-age or invalidity benefit entitlements by virtue of the derived entitlements of a wife

(d) the granting of increases of long-term invalidity, old-age, accidents at work and occupational disease benefits for an independent wife.

Equal pay

EEC Treaty – Article 119
Each member state shall during this first stage ensure and subsequently maintain the application of the principle that men and women should receive equal pay for equal work.

UK infringement of the Equal Pay Directive
This is a clear example of the process through which European equal opportunities legislation is implemented in member states and specifically, here in the UK. The EEC Council of Ministers issued a Directive on equal pay in February 1975, reinforcing and extending Article 119 of the Treaty of Rome. Article 1 of this Directive defines the principle of equal pay as meaning ' . . . for the same work or for work to which equal value is attributed, the elimination of all discrimination on the grounds of sex with regard to all aspects of and conditions of remuneration. In particular, where a job classification system is used for determining pay, it must be based on the same criteria for both men and women and so drawn up as to exclude any discrimination on the grounds of sex.'

Member states were given a year to implement fully the Equal Pay Directive. The UK did not do so, and faced infringement proceedings.

In *Commission of the European Communities v United Kingdom (1982)* the European Court of Justice ruled that the Equal Pay Act did not comply with the Equal Pay Directive because it failed to give an employee the right to claim equal pay with a person of the opposite sex for doing work of equal value in the same establishment where there is no system of job evaluation. The result was that the Act was amended to allow an employee to bring an equal pay claim in such circumstances.

If Europe remains the innovator in such legislation, this interactive process is likely to continue into the next century (see Chapter 7).

The development of equal opportunities in employment in the US

The concepts of equal employment opportunity, contract compliance and better use of women and minority ethnic groups in the workplace have been covered by regulation, administrative policy and legislation in the US for the last forty years.

1941: Franklin D Roosevelt barred discrimination against black workers in all federal government war contracts.

1943: this was expanded to cover all federal contractors.

1961: John Kennedy issued Executive Order 10925, which required the federal government to take 'affirmative action' to provide equal employment opportunity for minority ethnic workers. The Presidential Committee on Equal Employment Opportunity was established to develop rules, regulations and orders to oversee the implementation of the policy.

1964: the Civil Rights Act was passed in which Title VII prohibited employment discrimination, and gave the courts the authority to order 'affirmative action' in finding remedies for victims of discrimination.

1965: Lyndon Johnson issued Executive Order 11246 which prohibited discrimination in federal contract and made the Secretary of Labor responsible for administering enforcement.

1967: Executive Order 11375 expanded coverage of 11246 to include women.

1972: Congress passed the Equal Employment Act guaranteeing women freedom from employment discrimination.

1971: President Nixon introduced the regulations which govern the contract compliance field today and established the importance of affirmative action plans, the setting of goals and timetables, the formation of job classifications and the other major elements of current contract compliance enforcements.

1978: President Carter issued Executive Order 12067 restructuring the areas of government responsible for the overseeing of equal employment opportunity and federal contract compliance to make them more streamlined and accountable.

Thus two types of affirmative action have become government policy: the *administrative* strategy focussing on contract compliance and on the role of the US government in encouraging equal opportunity as an employer and contractor, and the *legislative/judicial* strategy focussing on the codifying of equal opportunity in employment and on the role of government as litigant on behalf of victims of discrimination.

US affirmative action has gained its strength through the interaction between these two strategies.

The approach of the Reagan administration to affirmative action and its possible effect on the future of equal opportunities in employment is discussed in Chapter 7. Until recently, however, it is true to say that the basic philosophy of the federal government on working towards a more equitable workplace had been consistent for the last twenty years.

In the past, American affirmative action policies have greatly influenced British equality legislation. This can be seen specifically in the formation of indirect discrimination legislation.

Indirect discrimination
The concept of indirect discrimination as a form of unlawful behaviour in the UK derives from the decision of the US Supreme Court in *Griggs v Duke Power Co*. This interpreted that Title VII of the Civil Rights Act 1964:

> 'prescribes not only discrimination but also practices that are fair in form, but discriminatory in operation. The touchstone is business necessity. If an employment practice which operates to exclude Negroes cannot be shown to be related to job performance, the practice is prohibited'.

The result of the Griggs case was to permit ethnic minorities, women, disabled people etc, to challenge any employment practice having a 'disparate impact' and to require the employer to defend such a practice by showing that it is necessary for business. The objective of Title VII was to 'achieve Equality of Employment opportunity and remove barriers that have operated in the past to favour an identifiable group of white employees over other employees.'

The UK Sex Discrimination Act consciously followed this model, renaming 'disparate impact' – indirect discrimination. Parallel wording is found in the definition of discrimination in the Race Relations Act 1976 and the case law decided under the one statute is regarded by the courts as precedent for the other.

The effectiveness of this indirect discrimination legislation in the UK is debatable. It is not known how many of the 233 successful complaints brought under the Race Relations Act up until the end of 1984 were based on indirect discrimination but the number of favourable decisions remains in single figures.

The weakest central aspect of European and UK discrimination law compared with US law is the statement that indirect discrimination may be justifiable on 'economic grounds'. This opens up a loophole as a cost justification can be found for most discriminatory practices.

In the US, as one American court put it:

> 'The sole permissible reason for discriminating against actual or prospective employees involves the individual's capability to perform the job effectively. This approach leaves no room for arguments regarding inconvenience, annoyance or even expense to the employer'.

The future impact of US anti-discrimination policy on the UK is examined in chapter 8.

References

1 BIRKETT K *and* WORMAN D, eds. *Getting on with disabilities: an employer's guide*. London, The Institute of Personnel Management, 1988.
   This has provided the main background for the section on disability legislation.
2 RUBENSTEIN, Michael. 'Discrimination: a guide to the relevant case law on race and sex discrimination and equal pay'. *Equal Opportunities Review*, 1988.
   A valuable source of information on EEC directives.
3 MARANO, Cynthia. 'Affirmative action in the United States: two decades of expanded opportunity'. Presented at a symposium on 'Equal opportunity through contract compliance'. London, February, 1986.
   The main source for information on US equal employment opportunities.

Chapter 3 Equal opportunities policy

The legislation outlined in chapter 2 established the broad frame-work within which equal opportunities policies should be developed. Before looking at the process of development, it is worth defining what equality of opportunity and an equal oppor-tunity policy are. A third question might also be posed – how is an equal opportunity policy different from established personnel practice? Some answers to these questions will be given below.

What is equal opportunity?

Ask this question in an interview situation and the response is usually something like: 'giving everyone a fair chance'. Take the question further by asking, 'how is this not so at present?' and the candidate will either elucidate handsomely on the finer prin-ciples of equal opportunity practice, or stutter nervously as one of their worst fears about the interview is realized.

In answer to the original question, however, it is possible to construct a number of models which provide an explanation. One such model outlines equal opportunity at three levels:

Level 1 – Equal opportunity as equal chance (non-discrimination)
This is synonymous with our hypothetical candidate's answer. In theory everyone does have an equal chance. 'Equal' in this case means 'the same'. I could, for instance, read in a newspaper one morning that a job is vacant in a particular company. In order to apply I need to visit the company's premises. I choose to do so, and on the way there discover that twenty other people, men and women, black and white, able-bodied and disabled have made exactly the same choice. We all arrive at the company at more or less the same time, and encounter a gatekeeper. The gatekeeper

has his own ideas as to who is suitable for the job (though he may not be able to articulate them) and only lets those people in who conform to his ideal. The question of whether his ideal is in any way relevant or reasonable is not one for his consideration; he *knows* what he thinks and what he thinks *must* be right. The potential for bias is enormous.

This illustrates the difficulty with the first level of equal opportunity: whilst in theory people do have the same chance, the reality is that discrimination will occur at some point. It may be lawful; it is also often unlawful. If our gatekeeper was only choosing to admit white able-bodied males because they were white able-bodied males, to the exclusion of all others, this would clearly be unlawful. In equal opportunity terms, there is no point in people having the same chance if there are unjustifiable barriers in place which restrict access for some.

Level 2 – Equal opportunity as equal access
Returning to our 'gatekeeper' analogy, let us assume that a process of enlightenment has taken place. Anyone who comes along gets in. In this instance not only can I get an interview – I may even get the job! This must be equal opportunity in action!

It could well be an improvement when those previously not having access begin to appear to do so. The next test to be applied, however, is: what jobs are the previously under-represented groups performing? What chance do they have of progressing? It is not difficult to find organizations with black, Asian or Chinese female secretaries; but how many of these are there in the boardroom, in the manager's office, as supervisors? It is still possible, even though the first level of discrimination has been removed, that the other unnecessary barriers will remain. More crucially, there is still no recognition of the history of discrimination which has affected the lives of many women, minority ethnic groups and people with disabilities – in particular the extent to which they will have had access to job and educational opportunities. (See chapter 7.)

Level 3 – Equal opportunity as an equal share
This level is the ideal. At level 3, not only is access and representation gained, but there is representation at every level. Account is taken of the history of particular groups, and particular measures taken to provide opportunities previously not available. In

this instance both the gatekeeper and the chair of the board might well be black women. The only criteria against which people discriminate in terms of recruitment, selection and promotion are lawful, justifiable and necessary.

An equal opportunities policy

Given this sort of analysis of equal opportunity, what meaning does it have when the word 'policy' is added to the end? Policy implies objective (an end product); objective implies strategy (a way of reaching that end product). An equal opportunities policy is a strategy, a programme of action. Objectives will vary from organization to organization, but in general they will feature *the elimination of unlawful discriminatory practices and the promotion of measures designed to combat the effects of past discrimination.*

For most organizations a lot of this can be summarized in one word – change. Changes in practices and procedures; changes in the profile of the workforces; maybe even changes to the 'culture' of the organization.

Introducing an equal opportunities policy
The reasons for introducing an equal opportunities policy need no rehearsal, and are shown in a practical sense in chapter 6. A more pertinent question is whether or not those who continue to mount arguments against their introduction will be able to maintain them in the future. As the starting point of an organization's strategy for introducing an equal opportunity policy, it is worth being clear about the reasons for doing so, and what will happen. Will it mean changing practices? What are the benefits? These and other key questions all need to be considered.

Where should one start? If equal opportunity programmes are considered in the context of bringing about organizational change, one person should have ultimate responsibility for the process: chief executive/managing director or chair of the board, for example. Unless an equal opportunity policy has the full, unequivocal backing of those most senior in the organization, it is unlikely to be effective. This is not to suggest that all that needs to be done is 'convince the boss and it will be OK'. There is usually a group of people at the top of an organization – they will all need to be similarly convinced.

Once the top management team becomes aware of the equal opportunity programme, everyone else must be told. Existing communication channels, in house magazines, publicity campaigns, and notice boards can all be used. Of particular importance will be trade unions, where they exist. A joint initiative for the initial information exercise may help to allay fears of 'management imposition'. Trade unions themselves are aware (at national level) of the need for equal opportunity policies. In unionized environments the process will almost certainly involve negotiation, and this should be encouraged.

The role of personnel
Where a personnel department exists, its role will be central to the successful implementation and communication of an equal opportunity policy, not least because the major areas of activity will be recruitment selection, training and development. Personnel will also have a continuing role in the monitoring and development of policies (see page 67). Some organizations choose to appoint a specialist with a specific equal opportunity brief (or a number of people to deal with the various issues, i.e. race, gender, disability, sexuality, etc.).

An important distinction needs to be drawn, however between *initial* and *eventual* ownership of equal opportunity policies, particularly in organizations where line managers from other functions are involved in personnel processes. The aim should be to enable *all* managers to 'own' equal opportunity policies, but a common error is that personnel staff appoint themselves (or are seen to appoint themselves) as 'sole guardians' of the principle.

This problem can be exacerbated where people are assigned specialist equal opportunity roles. Who takes responsibility if problems occur in implementing the policy and in its operation? If line managers simply refer matters to the personnel function, then the likelihood of marginalization and rejection of the policy is increased. This emphasizes the need for a clear and thorough communication process, fully involving line managers as well as personnel people. Another problem which arises with appointing equal opportunity specialists is that their presence is further 'proof' that equal opportunity practice is somehow different from ordinary personnel practice.

However, there are advantages. A decision to commit additional resources to equal opportunities as an issue by employing specialists can act as a sign of an organization's commitment. Equal opportunity specialists can also provide a good, initial, sometimes much needed, push to the implementation process.

The eventual aim, however, should be to ensure that personnel practice takes full account of equal opportunities considerations, and in this specialists should eventually work themselves out of a job. The ideal scenario is one where most of the information regarding implementation will originate from personnel, but where they fully involve and give responsibility to line managers for communicating and implementing the practical elements of an equal opportunities policy.

Monitoring and information
The supply of good quality information, in terms of detail and precision, is fundamental to the implementation and maintenance of an equal opportunities policy (EOP). Having a policy implies reaching stated objectives, and the old adage about not knowing where one is going without some idea of original destination is as true here as in any other area of policy. In order to set objectives, the starting point must be known. In the equal opportunity context this will involve obtaining information about the composition of the workforce in terms of ethnicity, gender, etc. In many organizations, obtaining census information becomes extremely problematic for two main reasons:

- people fail to see the need for the information

- fears/concerns and/or cynicism about its initial sincerity and eventual use.

This is often true when collecting information on ethnicity. Some white people feel that as well as such information not being relevant, it will lead to 'positive discrimination' in favour of ethnic minorities, which they will obviously react against. (The notion of positive discrimination is discussed in chapter 5.) Conversely, black people often feel that being asked to identify themselves as black will be used against them and prevent them from getting jobs. Both ethnic minorities and white people will often express concerns about the morality of 'classifying' people into one category or another. Race is a highly controversial issue and it is unlikely that attitude change will be achieved solely through the introduction of an EOP (though the role of training would have some effect on challenging assumptions). Cast iron assurances will have to be given in answer to the points raised, and additional stress put on the fact that evaluating the success of the policy is impossible unless this information is available, since part of the evaluation will involve seeing how things stand at different stages.

Obtaining information
As far as obtaining the information is concerned, a questionnaire is probably the most common method of collection. As well as ensuring quick, wide coverage, it also enables people to identify themselves – important from the view of accuracy.

A debate exists as to the propriety of self-classification as a means of obtaining data. This again focusses on the race issue. There are a number of facets to this:

- there is sometimes a lack of clarity as to exactly what 'ethnic origin' means. Is it the same as nationality? Is it place of birth? Colour of skin? Origin of parents or grandparents? The more options there are, the easier classification becomes. This can, however, lead to making the collection and analysis of data complex and unwieldy. All of the factors just outlined are relevant, but the essential point is that an individual's ethnic origin is whatever they consider it to be. Parameters often have to be set, but they should be sufficiently flexible to encompass most possibilities. The CRE's recently published guidelines on 'classifications' are a useful starting point.

- a point often made about monitoring in general, which also relates to self classification, is that it often can be seen as irrelevant – particularly by those deemed to be 'beneficiaries' of such action. By making someone's ethnic origin a focal point, particularly as far as the recruitment process is concerned, a sort of 'victimology' is created which runs counter to the concept of and therefore the likely acceptance of the 'spirit' of an equal opportunity policy. Clarity about the use of such information is helpful, but will not assist where misuse of it has clearly been demonstrated or is perceived.

Questionnaires can be followed up or supplemented by some form of management headcount. Once a complete picture is obtained, the profile can be updated by the section on application forms.

Another aspect of the debate mentioned earlier relates to the collection of ethnic monitoring data through application forms. One argument says that, given the extreme confidentiality of this information, access to it needs to be restricted to as few people as possible. This calls for an addition to the application forms, or at least a facility (eg a tear-off slip) which enables monitoring data to be separated from the general information. The general extension of this argument is that interviewers would not know the ethnic origin of candidates at the shortlisting stage, and would be therefore less susceptible to bias. In some instances candidates become completely anonymous with only job-related information (eg qualifications, work history, supporting information) being supplied. The personnel department then match applications to people and inform interviewers accordingly. In other instances, monitoring data forms remains an integral part of the application form.

There is no absolute rule which dictates that either approach is the right one. The decision as to which to use will to a certain extent depend upon some estimation of the likelihood of discrimination occurring on the basis of someone's race or gender at the shortlisting stage, which will in turn depend upon how much commitment, understanding, or awareness exists within the organization concerning equal opportunity issues in general.

This information can then be collected onto some form of central record – ideally, computerized. Other publications will talk in more detail about the specifics of computerization, but it is worth stating here that an investment in fairly sophisticated software is worthwhile from the point of view of the variety and precision of the information.

Making it work – review and maintenance
Having information to hand is obviously the key to making the EOP work; on the basis of this information, progress can be monitored, adjustments made and practices changed, and the ongoing process of EOP sustained. However, other factors are as important, and some of these will relate to day-to-day operations.

Targeting

This is a word which has become more frequently used recently in relation to EO than in the past. Its use is controversial, but at the heart of the controversy there seems to be a confusion between a 'target' and a 'quota'. A quota is an *absolute minimum*, usually related to some notion of proportion of the workforce. For instance, each organization over 20 employees is required by law to employ three per cent disabled people as a proportion of its total workforce. By absolute minimum, it means that there can be no negotiation or concession. Not meeting a quota is normally subject to some form of sanction or penalty. Except in the employment of registered disabled people, the use of quotas in employment practice is unlawful in the UK, since it involves the use of selection purely on grounds such as race or gender, which is also unlawful (except where absolutely necessary, i.e. GOQ provisions).

A target is a *guideline* – possibly also related to proportion. It is not absolute, more an indication of whether or not satisfactory progress is being made, in the same way that a sales target might be used to assess the performance of a sales person. No legal penalties or sanctions can be imposed through not meeting targets. Since the setting of targets in no way contradicts the principle of selecting the most suitable person for the job, they are not in any way unlawful.

In setting targets the following principles are worth bearing in mind:

- analyze jobs in terms of grade, function, level etc and establish the representation of ethnic minorities, women, people with disabilities

- establish a rationale for your target or desired outcome, eg three per cent disabled people or a representation of ethnic minorities in terms relative to their presence in the local area

- set a timescale – months, maybe years. Take into account the nature of the job and the likelihood of attracting those from the under-represented group into those jobs, given past rates of applying, human resource, planning information etc

- obtain regular reports showing what progress has been made.

The regularity will depend on your timescale but quarterly or half yearly reports should be useful

Where it is found that insufficient progress is being made, *investigate*. Examine practices: gather detailed evidence from other people involved in selection/promotion decisions, particularly in relation to candidates from the under-represented groups. Changes to practices may well be necessary; alternatively, some form of positive action may be required (see chapter 5).

Training
It is clearly good practice for an employer to provide training for those staff involved in the selection process – particularly interviewing. The need for training is given added weight through EO considerations. Training should go beyond merely looking at legislative provisions: additional ground to be covered includes the examination of job requirements to ensure that unlawful and unnecessary criteria are eliminated when establishing requirements in terms of job and person, and looking at elements of interviewing practice to identify and help eliminate assumptions, stereotypes and techniques which act to the detriment of minority ethnic people, women and people with disabilities at the interview stage.

Cost
Chapter 1 looked at the belief that 'equal opportunity makes good business sense' and concluded that one of the reasons why EOPs are not more widely in evidence is because of the financial cost. Equal opportunity costs time and costs money: time in collating information, negotiating and communicating the policy, and in assessing the results, and money spent on publicity, introducing new systems, new equipment and sometimes new people, almost certainly in recruitment advertising. This is where large organizations with well-established personnel procedures have an advantage, as it is a much smaller proportional cost to supplement and adapt existing procedures and databases than it is to introduce totally new systems.

It is arguable that the organizations to whom the cost implications will be greatest will be small firms who are growing. They may have a small or emerging personnel function which will need to be expanded and systematized, and to introduce written guidelines and staff training procedures. It is, however, also arguable that this is the optimum time to introduce equal opportunity policies, when there is no organizational inertia resisting change, and when development money will have been already allocated. The short-term view suggests that something which involves an investment of this order cannot be good business sense. The flaw in this, obviously, is that it is a short-term view. Long-term planning is essential for business survival. Given the predicted demographic changes, firms can no longer afford *not* to have fair recruitment policies, good prospects of advancement and flexible working schemes. If they do not have good working conditions, potential and existing employees will go elsewhere, and the financial loss in terms of productivity and quality of service will be infinitely greater than the cost of introducing and running fairer policies. The question will in future be not whether one can afford to, but whether one can afford not to.

Checklist

The preceding pages give an outline of the steps that need to be taken in implementing, maintaining and reviewing an EOP. Prescription is difficult, as organizations differ widely; individual decisions based on individual needs and objectives will prevail. As a summary, however, the following should act as a checklist for the implementation processes:

- obtain information – workforce profiles, response analyses. Establish the starting point

- get the commitment to action – from the top down, and from the bottom up

- set targets – yardsticks for measuring progress

- review regularly

- communicate with all staff – say what's happening, why, how it will affect them, how they will benefit

- train people – particularly those involved in recruiting.

Chapter 4 Equal opportunity and employment practice

In Chapter 2, a legislative framework for equal opportunity was established. Yet the practical application of the theory is as important and this chapter is concerned with how this happens. Each stage of the employment process will be examined from an equal opportunity viewpoint. The intention here is not to 're-invent the wheel', merely to provide assistance to practitioners reviewing their own procedures and practices.

It would be inappropriate to suggest an 'ideal procedure'. Different organizations adopt different processes to suit their own needs. An equal opportunity policy must fit within these, and form a central 'plank' of personnel policy, in order to be effective. This is not to suggest, however, that personnel managers should not be prepared to make changes where necessary.

The recruitment process

Recruitment, here, refers to those processes leading to the point at which a range of candidates are available to choose from, i.e. when a shortlist is being drawn up. From an equal opportunity point of view, there are a number of clearly identifiable stages:

1 Identifying job requirements – job descriptions/person specifications

Establishing job descriptions and person specifications need not mean drafting pages outlining job content in minute detail (although organizations using analytical job evaluation schemes may be used to this). Job descriptions ought, however, to outline the overall purpose of the job and the major tasks. The person specification is derived from these, this being an outline of the skills and qualities the job-holder will possess. It is best to start with a blank sheet and identify in specific terms what is necessary. Things to think about are:

- qualifications – are they absolutely necessary or an unnecessary barrier? This is particularly true when recruiting junior staff (school leavers, etc). Imposing a blanket requirement for a certain number of GCSEs, without any consideration as to whether the job actually requires them, needs to be carefully thought through. There is considerable evidence (see Chapter 7) to suggest that minority ethnic children and girls underachieve in the education system – not through any inherent lack of ability, but through the effects of discrimination. An insistence on qualifications in the recruitment process could compound the discrimination suffered. Equally as pernicious (and controversial) is the apparent insistence on recruiting graduates for many positions. This is not to question the appropriateness of graduate recruitment *per se*, so long as whatever is being sought can primarily (or exclusively) be found within graduates. How often is this *really* the case, though?

- physical requirements – is a level of physical strength required or are there aids available?

Another key question is the balance between *essential* and *desirable* requirements within person specifications. In most cases, desirable requirements are included for use in the recruitment process where large numbers of applicants are expected. In some circumstances, however, the inclusion of non-essential requirements can act as an unnecessary barrier – eg, how often is an awareness of equal opportunity issues included as an aspect of selection criteria?

2 *Advertising*
Does this happen?! Some organizations rarely (or perhaps never) advertise positions, perhaps because of a policy of internal promotions. This in itself is not unlawful; but the question of whether or not such a practice constitutes indirect discrimination is worth considering. If an organization is solely or mainly comprised of white males (or white men and women) and positions are filled by the existing workforce, opportunities to employ (for instance)

a minority ethnic person do not exist. If adopting such a practice can be justified in terms of job performance, then there is no difficulty according to the law. How often, again, is this really the case?

There are two other important issues here: how the advertisement is worded and where it is placed. In the advertisement itself, a key word is *encouragement*. Section 38 of the Race Relations Act and Section 48 of the Sex Discrimination Act allow for the encouragement of under-represented groups (under-representation in this context refers to the position at a particular level or in a particular occupation in the twelve-month period prior to advertising). Encouragement is all that is allowed: an advertisement should still convey the impression that applications are welcomed from all sectors of the population, unless being of a particular sex or ethnic group is a genuine occupational qualification.

In relation to *placement*, it is worth thinking about a wide cast of the advertising net. A rule that applies in a general sense also applies in equal opportunity terms. If professional staff were being sought, an obvious place to advertise would be the relevant professional journals. If the aim, in equal opportunity terms, is to attract more minority ethnic people, using the black press might well prove useful – as well as informing the readers of that organization's commitment to equal opportunities. A cautionary note, however – do not be disappointed if there is no instant response from one advert, or even from a series of adverts over a few months. Thirty years of mistrust built up through discrimination will not be broken down easily – some perseverance will be needed.

Selection

The advertisement, if effective, will elicit a range of candidates. At this point the decision-making process to choose the successful one begins. It is here that equal opportunity considerations assume most importance. Again, there are a number of clearly identifiable stages.

Shortlisting
Unless all who apply are automatically seen, some process for sifting out unsuitable candidates will need to be adopted. At

this point, the criteria appearing in the person specification are employed, and shortlisting should be carried out using these as a basis. Candidates will normally have responded to these requirements, and to assess their suitability on the basis of completely different qualities, or on additional ones would not only be unfair but illegal. It is helpful to have all the information presented in the same way. Using the same application form for all candidates, rather than asking for CVs, is the easiest way to achieve this.

Selection tests
In general, selection tests are useful in terms of ensuring objective decisions. Person specifications ask for the skills needed to do the job. Using tests to assess those skills is far more reliable than assuming that someone from a particular background with particular experiences possesses what is required. So if, for instance, written and verbal communication skills to a particular level are needed, an exercise can be devised which actually assesses these things – ideally in an environment similar to the job situation. Group exercises, numeric and verbal reasoning tests and simulations, properly designed and validated, can assist in providing better quality information upon which to base recruitment decisions.

As far as the question of culture and gender bias is concerned, it is probably fair to say that widely-used tests will inevitably incorporate an element of bias if the norms upon which they are based are suitably specific. This is particularly true of personality tests: if the test population is white, middle-class and male, the norms established will reflect those values. Norms for groups other than white males may be difficult to obtain, and cannot be guaranteed to produce results significantly different from those existing. Nevertheless, where it is found that the use of selection tests appear adversely to affect minority ethnic applicants and women, in the sense that they consistently appear to fare less well than their white, male counterparts, then it could well be that culture bias is a factor. In this case the tests should not be used.

The IPM have produced a code on occupational testing. This is outlined in more detail in Appendix 2.

Interviews
Despite the long-established unreliability of interviews, it is still the case that the majority of organizations will not only use them,

but will base their recruitment decisions upon information gained through the interviews more than through any other part of the selection process. Many aspects of interviews could be subject to scrutiny: these are the main considerations:

• solo or panel? Many organizations will recruit staff on the basis of an interview with one person. Whilst this of itself may not mean that discrimination will occur, having more than one person playing an equal role during an interview will at least provide varying perspectives. Properly trained, they will increase the effectiveness of the interview – not by eliminating bias completely, but through having to recognize it.

• an interview is a process of social interaction. If you walk into a room and meet someone not known to you, how do you feel? If you identify that person as being similar to you, then initial tensions disappear more quickly than if the person is quite different. These feelings are the same for both the interviewer and the interviewee. What if the differences are unreconcilable? A man interviewing a woman (or vice versa); a white man interviewing an Afro-Caribbean, Asian or Chinese woman? Consider the possible impact upon each party in the interaction – positive as well as negative. If it is accepted that interviews are (for most people) anxious experiences, responsibility for reducing anxiety lies principally with the interviewers. Having someone whom candidates can at least visually identify with will help in this process. This is not an argument for including people of minority ethnic origin and women on panels as a token gesture – whoever participates has to play a full role.

• the information gained at interviews will be elicited through questions, where there is as much room for bias as anywhere else. Some points to consider are:

  – would you ask a man about childcare arrangements?

  – would you ask a white candidate how they would deal with racially hostile attitudes?

  – would you ask a man whether they intended to get married, or about their personal relationships?

With a little adaptation these all become familiar questions –

but for the wrong reasons. Note that asking questions like these is not in itself unlawful; but asking men about childcare, or white people about racist attitudes, is not a solution. The main point is whether they are relevant to ask in an interview. Relying on answers to questions such as these would almost certainly amount to indirect discrimination.

Equal opportunities within employment

It is important to remember that as well as focussing attention on equal opportunity at the recruitment stage, there is a need to look at what happens to people already there. Adopting, implementing or reinforcing equal opportunity policies is, for most organizations, an issue of change. The process should be managed with no less effort than any other change issue.

The induction process
The starting point for this is the induction process. Exactly what takes place during induction will vary between organizations. Some initial questions to be asked are: to what extent is an awareness and an understanding of equal opportunity issues a central feature? Having an hour or two, or even a morning within the induction programme is all very well, but is it clear what this means to the individual? What expectations should staff have of the organization and vice versa? How much clarity is there about who 'owns' equal opportunities – the personnel department, or everyone? Is it seen as an addition to general policy and practice or the foundation of it? Who delivers the session – the induction trainer or a 'specialist'?

How each organization answers these questions will vary according to the stage of development and awareness of equal opportunity issues, but they are well worth asking.

Ideally, the implementation of an equal opportunity policy will be based on effective communication. This needs to be maintained. The induction process will inform new staff: what about existing staff?

The two main areas in developing a broader awareness of equal opportunities amongst existing staff are:

• other training courses: similar questions to those posed above can be asked of training courses generally within the organization

- day-to-day line management – particularly one-to-one super-visions – can be useful for focussing on individual attitudes and behaviours. There is a fairly obvious, and major, implication here for the way in which managers are developed and trained.

Training

Positive action measures (see chapter 5) may mean that an apparently disproportionate amount of time, effort and resources will be focussed on previously under-represented groups. There should be no apologizing for this. Rather than being seen as preferential treatment it should be explained as remedying the effect of previous disadvantage.

Having said that, while much attention has been paid to the needs of minority ethnic groups and women, white males, very much the butt of criticism in equal opportunity terms as being the holders of power, will need as much education about their role in ensuring that equal opportunities happens on a day-to-day basis. This is not about a loss of power and status, but rather about an equitable distribution of it.

Promotion

Chapter 3 referred to the importance of monitoring and information; again, the needs continue beyond the initial stages of recruitment and workforce monitoring.

Promotion systems are worthy of particular examination, not only the systems themselves, but also the outcomes they produce. Are they discriminatory in effect? For instance, promotion which is based on seniority, i.e. length of service, can often have a discriminatory effect. The question to be asked is how diverse was the workforce in terms of ethnicity and gender five, ten or twenty years ago? If length of service is an explicit or implicit requirement for promotion, and the workforce ten years ago was predominantly white and male, then those eligible will also be white and male.

Justifiability is a key issue here. If somebody with that length of service has clearly demonstrable achievements which are not available through any other route, and their requirement is justifiable in terms of job performance, then it may be worth retaining seniority as one factor in assessing suitability for promotion. It need not, however, be a deciding factor, and it should be remembered that where using seniority as the main criteria is not justifiable, it is potentially unlawful.

Even after reviewing potential pitfalls such as these, and taking account of resource planning issues, it is useful just to look at pure outcomes. How many minority ethnic people are being promoted? How many women? How many people with disabilities? What are the success rates, i.e. the proportion promoted as a percentage of those groups in the organization as a whole?

Employee turnover

A key indicator of the success or otherwise of the implementation and maintenance of an equal opportunity policy is the impact it has on employee turnover. There is, again, a need for information here. Having turnover information available in terms of race, gender and disability can be quite revealing. Detail is important, though, as an analysis which showed that more women were leaving the organization than men would on its own be misleading. The majority of those women could well have left for positive rather than negative reasons, possibly as a direct consequence of some positive action measures. This, in turn, raises an issue for organizations about being able to utilize the skills that it has enabled its staff to acquire.

Exit interviews are a good way of acquiring this type of information. There can, however, be some very practical difficulties with implementing a general exit interview programme. One reason may be the scale of larger organizations, but as important is the quality of the information obtained, which in turn is related to who is obtaining it, and how 'safe' the employee feels in giving it out.

The importance of having reliable information on leavers takes on an additional dimension when looked at from an equal opportunity perspective. It serves to reinforce a fundamental point concerning equal opportunity in organizations. It is a *management* issue. If an organization is able to recruit people from minority ethnic communities and women where it was unable to before, but those same people leave as quickly as they were recruited, questions should be asked about the way they were managed and were able to manage themselves.

Complementary awareness raising

There is no doubt that equal opportunity policies have crept up the order of the human resources management agenda, particularly in recent years. There is equally little doubt that the majority of organizations have much progress to make in this area.

From the point of view of the personnel profession, the Institute of Personnel Management has a key role to play. Being the most reliable and objective arbiter of professional standards, IPM has taken a lead, and should continue to be seen to take a lead in this area. The publication of their Equal Opportunities Code and the recent upgrading of the Standing Committee on Equal Opportunity to national status are important steps in this respect.

They cannot, however, do it alone. The relevant statutory agencies – the CRE and EOC – are also important, not only from the point of view of promotion of equal opportunity, but also enforcement. One of the most fundamental questions in the field is the role of legislation and enforcement agencies and the extent to which a strengthening of the law would actually bring about the desired outcomes. There is a view which states that the CRE and EOC ought, in fact, to restrict themselves to enforcement (allied to a strengthening in the law) and leave the promotion to someone else.

Exactly who that someone else should be is difficult to say. In a perfect world, individual employers would each take on the responsibility for introducing, maintaining and developing equal opportunities. However, this is not a perfect world. Specialist organizations, with an existing track record in the fields of equal opportunities in employment practices (see chapter 9 on resources) is another option. The maxim about equal opportunity making good business sense needs to be proved to be true. What better method than for organizations to prove it to each other?

Chapter 5 The proactive approach

The last chapter ended by drawing attention to the amount of progress which needs to be made in most UK organizations in implementing equal opportunity policies. The legislative framework, defining statutory requirements, was outlined in chapter 2.

But this provides an absolute minimum. There is a great deal more which can be done, and which organizations showing a commitment to equal opportunity policies would want and need to do in order to make them work effectively. In introducing these policies, the need for them is first adopted by senior management. Personnel is then called upon to research and plan their implementation.

Personnel will need to look at the compulsory, legislative requirements and make sure they fulfil them. They will start to look at their recruitment and employment policies, but may come up against a brick wall. How can they encourage more women, more minority ethnic groups, and more disabled people into their workforce without being accused of discriminating against men, white people and the able-bodied?

It is the difference between widening the opportunity net and showing favours; the difference between good personnel practice and over redressing the balance to produce a new kind of inequality.

This chapter looks at how to widen the opportunity net. It makes clear the distinction between positive discrimination, which is illegal, and positive action, and outlines different kinds of flexible working. It introduces ways of raising awareness amongst staff already in the organization as a way of creating a deeper understanding and more positive environment for equal opportunities policies.

Positive discrimination and positive action

'Positive discrimination' describes the situation where people are appointed to jobs on grounds other than those which are job-related. This phrase may be used where the appointee is from a minority ethnic group, or is a woman or disabled. The principal reason they are appointed is because of their race, gender or disability; their proven ability to carry out the job may be of secondary importance. Because of this the phrase has become a loaded one and closely associated with the groups referred to above. For instance, it is rarely used in situations where, as an outcome, a white male is employed.

Discrimination on grounds of race or gender (except where a genuine occupational qualification exists) at the point of selection is, and will probably remain, unlawful in this country (see Chapter 2). Yet a link is still made between equality targets (confused with quotas) and 'positive discrimination'. The problems with positive discrimination are many, but two are worth dwelling on here:

(i) *the 'setting up to fail' syndrome* – where a minority ethnic individual or woman is appointed on the grounds of their colour or gender rather than their ability to do the job in question, there is a high risk of failure. This is particularly true where they are the first in a particular job or grade and are subject to additional pressures. Combining this with traditional resistance to make such appointments, two outcomes are likely: all the negative stereotypes will have been seen to be confirmed and, therefore, no such 'risks' will be taken again.

(ii) *perceptions of positive discrimination* – even where the appointment is made on job related grounds, perception of 'positive discrimination' can still exist. The knowledge (or even suspicion) that such practices are being adopted will undermine the credibility and the success of any equal opportunity initiative – particularly disappointing where major efforts have been made to innovate.

'Positive action' is completely different. Its starting point is a recognition that each individual has different need (see Chapter 1). Where, however, there is a common experience based, for instance, on race or gender, this individual experience will have a common basis. For instance, minority ethnic children may experience conscious and unconscious prejudice during their education which causes them to underachieve. A recognition of this will lead to a programme of positive action. There are other aspects which underline the need for positive action. These are related to experience and lack of management.

Discrimination in society has deprived minority ethnic groups and women of opportunities which may in turn mean that they will not have acquired the experience considered necessary to perform a particular job. Alternatively, it may well be that rather than lacking the necessary experience, particular groups may just not be applying for particular jobs. In this case, a degree of encouragement will be required. Both the 1975 SDA and the 1976 RRA permit encouragement through the way jobs are advertised, to counter this. Lack of experience depends much more on providing training to bring people up to a level at which they can apply for jobs.

An important point is that positive action does not occur at the point of selection. Selection is still made on the basis of the best candidate for the job. The impact of positive action is felt during the recruitment process and then in the operation of employment practices. For instance, it is permissible to be selective in choosing people to attend positive action courses: in particular, S.37 of the RRA 1976 allows organizations suitably designated by the Department of Employment to be specific in advertising to attract people from under-represented groups. Under this section they can also be specific in their selection for attendance on training courses designed to equip participants with the skills necessary to compete for jobs in particular areas. Awareness training is another example of positive action.

Confusion between positive discrimination and positive action
Why is there confusion between the two concepts? In order to treat people equally in terms of outcome it is necessary to account for different needs, and this is true regardless of race or gender. Fears that 'preferential treatment' runs counter to the whole notion of equality abound in this area. At a sub-conscious level, however, fears often exist that correcting the effects of past discrimination in effect amounts to a surrendering of power – a loss of the 'share of the pie'. In reality, the 'pie' was historically

unequally distributed, but this is the situation that people have come to accept as normal. This in turn leads to the perception that reallocating the share is preferential treatment. The need to communicate clearly the aims and intentions of an equal opportunity policy is perhaps more clearly illustrated here than in any other area.

Awareness training

Awareness training is, quite simply, training which aims to make one set of people aware of the needs and abilities of another set of people.

In this book it is used in terms of developing an organizational culture which is open to groups of people who traditionally have not been represented at all levels of their organization. This includes minority ethnic groups, women and the disabled, although there is male awareness training which helps men to explore their own conditioning. Awareness training, therefore can have a secondary function: to enable a particular group to understand the basis of their own conditioning and actions and, if necessary, to attempt to redress them.

The use of awareness training
Awareness training can be used at any time during the introduction or implementation of equal opportunity policies, and can range from small informal discussion groups, to more structured sessions using videos, tapes and set discussion topics, to external training courses. Appendix 3 gives more details about the growth and content of awareness training.

The outcomes of awareness training in organizational terms should be to enable staff to work with maximum effectiveness, with minimum conflict, to ensure that each individual, of whatever race or sex, is respected for his/her beliefs and to ensure that everybody has equal prospects of advancement.

Awareness training should be closely tied in with the operation of equal opportunity policies within an organization. It should develop a greater receptivity to and understanding of the need for these policies, and should encourage each individual to evaluate their own behaviour, and to understand that they are each part of the same organization.

It should also enable each of the groups to develop confidence through mutual support. Appendix 3 shows how women can benefit from assertiveness training, self-development programmes, networking and the use of role models.

The resources section at the end of this book gives details of videos and training organizations which can help in the various forms of awareness training.

Flexibility in work

There are a variety of flexible working patterns which have been used more widely in the USA than in Britain, which particularly benefit women – with dependent younger and older relatives – but also those approaching retirement, and those men who want to take on more domestic responsibilities.

Why change?
The reasons for the shift towards greater flexibility in work include pressure from a workforce which has a higher proportion of women employees feeling the stress of the demands of family and work, and changing attitudes to work amongst employees who value leisure time as well as a satisfying work career. There is also pressure as the organization (see chapter 8) needs to be able to respond rapidly to change and to adjust from being in a production-based economy to a service-based economy. This means it needs to recruit, train and keep a highly skilled, flexible, mobile workforce of 'trained' employees. In the UK Joanna Foster, chair of the Equal Opportunities Commission, points out that role models are changing away from the workaholic superman or superwoman[1]. On the annual recruiting drives around universities, some organizations are finding that 50 per cent of the best graduates are now women. She has also noticed that it is the organizations which are addressing self-development, career and life planning, career break and childcare schemes which are the most attractive to new recruits. For instance, local authorities employ 1.6 million women, which is 17 per cent of all working women. Almost one million of these are in part-time jobs.

Employers are recognizing that where flexible work arrangements are not available, a worker with family responsibilities who is kept to a rigid working pattern may go absent, may conduct personal business on company time, and may ultimately leave their job.

Flexible working patterns

Flexitime
This refers to a work schedule which permits flexible starting and finishing times within limits set by the employer, but still requires a standard number of hours, usually 40, during a 5-day week, within a given time period. A core time, for instance between 10.00 am and 4.00 pm, will be defined for all employees. A survey carried out in the USA for the American Management Association found that 35 per cent of respondents offered flexitime.

Work at home
This is proliferating with the expanded use of computers. Telecommuting, telework and telecomputing all enable employees to work off-site while electronically linked to the office through a computer.

Regular part-time employment
This means less full-time work but which ideally includes job security and all other rights available to full-time workers, eg promotion. Parts of the financial sector and the Civil Service support this type of part-time work.

Compressed work week
This is a 40-hour week which is compressed into fewer than five days. The most common formulae are 4 days/10 hours, 3 days/12 hours, 4–5 days/9 hours.

Job sharing
This is a form of regular part-time work in which two people voluntarily share the responsibilities of one full-time position, with the salary and benefits shared accordingly.

Phased retirement programmes
These allow workers to reduce their work time and to retire gradually over a period of years. Employees usually assume regular part-time status.

Worksharing
This is an alternative to lay-offs, in which an organization's work-force temporarily reduces its hours and salary.

Voluntary reduced work time programmes
These are time/income trade-off arrangements which allow full-time employees to reduce their work hours for a specified period of time with a corresponding reduction in pay. There is a defined process for return to full-time status.

In the UK, employers of job sharers include the BBC, the Stock Exchange, the House of Commons, the Home Office, and there are many others. The most common arrangement is for each sharer to work two and a half days a week, but sharers can also work mornings or afternoons, or alternate weeks. Kent County Council define each job-share teaching role as a 1.1 full-time post, with the extra 0.5 for each sharer to be used as liaison time, and not for class contact time. The job-share scheme is available on all grades except head teacher posts.
   Job-sharing brings advantages to employers such as one job benefiting from two people's different skills and experience. There is also:

- increased flexibility

- peak period cover

- less absenteeism

- continuity during holidays and sick leave.

Special leave

Maternity leave
Statutory maternity leave stretches over 29 weeks at full pay. It can be taken any time after the completion of twenty eight weeks of pregnancy and within 6 months of the birth. This applies to employees who have completed two years of service with their current employer. Employers are, however, free to extend maternity leave beyond the statutory minimum, possibly on a reduced pay basis.

Paternity leave
This is an agreed length of leave (eg 20 days) which varies from organization to organization. It can be taken within one year of the birth of the baby. In some European countries paternity leave is a statutory obligation.

Leave of absence
This refers to an authorized period of time away from work without loss of employment rights, and may be paid or unpaid.

Extended leave
This is particularly important to minority ethnic groups, to enable individuals to visit relatives overseas. Company policies vary widely and may be informal and discretionary. Most organizations apply a service qualification to eligibility, the majority varying between six months and two years. The length of leave granted is between one and two months. In most cases, extended leave is built up from a combination of paid annual leave, often carried over more than one year, and unpaid leave.

Before employers grant extended leave, the reasons for it may come under scrutiny.

Career break schemes
These allow employees taking a career break for domestic reasons to return to employment at the same status at which they left. Posts will be protected for a specified length of time (commonly five–seven years) provided that the returner undertakes a period of work each year (weeks rather than months), and attends in-service training before returning.

In the UK, career break schemes of seven years' duration are supported by the CBI. 'It makes sense for businesses to offer highly skilled women the chance of returning to their jobs after pregnancy'.[2] Organizations such as Barclays, National Westminster Bank, Midland, Esso, Marconi, the Cabinet Office, the Inland Revenue, British Gas, the electricity supply industry and Kent Local Education Authority offer career break schemes.

Religious holidays
These are often taken out of annual leave entitlement or, where flexitime systems are in operation, through a build-up of leave. Some firms grant unpaid leave.

Prayer time
This can be fitted into existing flexitime systems or through the use of break periods.

Facilities

Creches or day nurseries
These may be state-funded, privately run or set up by a particular organization for the children of their employees. They take young children aged from six weeks to four years, and usually open at 8.00 am and stay open until 6.00 or 7.00 pm.

Nursery provision
Nursery provision is a logical development to day nurseries but is intended for children from three years up to school age. Where state provided, nurseries are often linked into local primary school provision.

Play schemes
These are available for schoolchildren for after school hours and holidays. Some are run by local authorities, both for employees and residents in the area; increasingly professions which are experiencing skills shortages are starting to consider sponsoring play scheme arrangements.

Facilities for the disabled
These are aimed at enabling physically disabled people to gain access to premises and to use equipment with ease. Typically they consist of ramps into buildings, lifts with buttons which are accessible from a wheelchair and widened toilets for wheelchair access.

References

1   FOSTER, Joanna. 'Balancing work and the family: divided loyalties or constructive partnership'. *Personnel Management*. September 1988.
2   THOMAS, Rod. *The Times*. 12 March 1988.

Chapter 6 Good practice in the public and private sector

Both public and private sector organizations have been involved in introducing equal opportunities policies over the last few years, and this chapter examines that process on a practical level. As examples of the public sector, some local authorities have introduced policies which have been castigated in the popular press as being the preserve of extremists and 'left-wing loonies', fuelling a somehow malevolent 'race relations industry' and extreme feminism.

Yet we have seen how equality of opportunity makes sense, both for the organization itself and for its employees. Over the last few years, some private sector organizations have also grasped the nettle fairly and squarely and made very active attempts to ensure that their entry requirements and career prospects offer equality both in opportunity and outcome.

Organizations which have taken steps along the road towards equal opportunities have often done so because someone in that organization feels a real, active commitment to the *principle* of making opportunities available to all. This, as the following case studies show, is often a member of the senior management team. Without a sincere belief in equality, the policy itself will be empty and mechanistic.

Different ways of constructing and implementing the policies depend on local circumstances, the needs of the organization and the energy of the staff involved. The policies are tailored to particular needs, but at the same time have a number of similarities between them, and this is because they address similar needs perhaps to attract more employees to the organization, or a sense of social responsibility to work with, and put something back into, the communities of which they are a part. The needs may be, in the service sector, to make their visible operations acceptable to the population in their locality.

None of the organizations mentioned here are being held up as perfect examples. The introduction of equal opportunities policies is an ongoing process and few, if any, employers would claim to have achieved a perfect model.

Most of the information in this chapter has been drawn from the organization's own booklets, from conversations and interviews with equal opportunities staff and from magazine articles. What the information shows is that there are elements of good practice in equal opportunities which have been found to work and which can be adopted and adapted to suit the needs of other organizations.

The public sector: the BBC

The BBC has 29,700 employees in total at a large number of different work bases. 25 per cent of its programmes are contracted out to independent companies.

In order to function, the BBC has devolved to Directorates, each of which has responsibility for all its functions, eg personnel, finance. The head of each of these Directorates come together in the Board of Management.

Policy statement
'The BBC's policies are based on equal opportunity for all. This applies to external recruitment, internal appointments, terms of employment, conditions of service and opportunities for training and promotion, irrespective of sex, marital status, creed, colour, race or ethnic origin, and the BBC is committed to the development and promotion of such equality of opportunity. Staff who believe they have been denied equality of opportunity may pursue their complaint through the appeals and grievances procedures, as may be appropriate.'

History of equal opportunities
In 1926 the BBC adopted the principle of equal pay; in 1973 limitations on the recruitment and promotion of women were removed. An equal opportunities statement was drawn up shortly afterwards in collaboration with the unions which was revised in

1983. In 1981, an equal opportunities committee was set up to monitor the effectiveness of the equal opportunities policy.

Despite this interest in equal opportunities, in 1982 only 21.9 per cent of middle managers and 7.2 per cent of heads of department were women. Against this background, staff were pressing for increases in opportunity and there was increasing concern that the growth in numbers of minority ethnic people in the general workforce wasn't being reflected in the BBC. In 1985, the Board of Governors asked for information on why women hadn't progressed further, and in 1986 they asked for further recommendations on implementing equal opportunities, but specifically related to minority ethnic people. Issues of disabilty and employment were also included briefly.

In 1987, the newly-appointed Equal Opportunities Officer produced an internal report recommending changes. These recommendations have formed the basis for activities over the last two years. In short, the report suggested action in the following areas: raising awareness, investing in staff, training people to make equal opportunities work, monitoring and publicizing the results.

What makes the policy active?
The BBC is committed to developing and promoting equality of action and implementation of the policy is a stated objective of its five year plan. The BBC aims to ensure that its managers take responsibility for the policy; part of this strategy involves the appointment of dedicated Equal Opportunities Officers who work with their managements to bring about change. There are now six EOOs (two job-sharing) working within Television, Radio, World Service, News and Current Affairs, Engineering and corporate departments such as Finance and Policy and Planning. A further Equal Opportunities Officer has been appointed to develop employment and training initiatives for disabled people. The equal opportunity strategy reflects the current structure of the BBC, with responsibility for policy implementation vested in the senior line management of each directorate.

The BBC's approach has been to find ways of involving managers directly in developing its equal opportunities initiatives. Groups of key decision makers, including the equal opportunities officers, have been formed (Directorate Implementation Groups) to advise on and support directorate action plans and priorities.

Employment practices

The annual review of staff performance, the use of 'attachments' to give experience in new areas within the BBC, job-sharing, part-time working, career breaks, maternity leave and extended leave for overseas visits all provide an increasing flexibility. A 60-place nursery catering for babies to pre-school is being set up in conjunction with the BBC's building developments in West London at White City.

To raise awareness, equal opportunities booklets for staff and management have been prepared and equal opportunities training for managers, using a combination of external consultants and internal staff, is well established. Equal opportunities is now a regular item at all local consultation meetings and there is regular coverage in the staff newspaper of equality issues, from flexible working arrangements to positive action schemes.

The ethnic monitoring procedures, which previously had only been used at the recruitment stage, were extended in 1987 to look at the ethnic composition of the workforce as a whole. This will therefore show patterns of career progression and areas where there is under-representation of minority ethnic groups. The BBC opted to collect this data from staff directly and prepared an information pack for each member of staff. The information in the pack, set out in question and answer form, was to raise the awareness of BBC equal opportunities policy and equality issues generally. Managers received supplementary information to enable them to carry out departmental briefings: *Why is this exercise being carried out?* There was extensive consultation with the trade unions and publicity in the staff newspaper. The exercise had the total support of the trade unions throughout and they carried out their own vigorous publicity through other channels.

Disability issues are discussed with unions at a sub-committee of the equal opportunities committee. The development of policies includes work experience schemes, environmental issues (eg access and evacuation) and awareness training.

Training courses

The BBC has introduced some very specifically targeted training courses, aimed to encourage women and members of minority ethnic groups to consider areas in which they are under-represented. For instance, there is an eight day intensive 'Operational Awareness' course, started with money from the European

Commission's Directorate of Employment, Social Affairs and Education through the EOC who approached the BBC. This enables women to gain some knowledge of the technical side of broadcasting. Designation under Section 37 of the Race Relations Act has been gained to provide radio journalist training and television reporter training for people of Asian and Afro-Caribbean origin. These schemes will cost £½ million over an 18 month–2 year period and provide six bursaries for each category, funded by trusts set up by the BBC. Training will consist of a mixture of formal training and work experience.

The Anniversary Training Fund was established to set up a television broadcasting course aimed at people who have been unemployed for six months or more. This was in order to celebrate 50 years of television. To date, 50 per cent of the trainees have come from minority ethnic groups.

A collaborative office skills course was run at Fullemploy Lambeth with BBC input and funded by North Peckham Task Force. It provided work experience at the BBC and seven of the trainees gained employment.

Outreach
Open evenings for Asian and Afro-Caribbean communities are held at regional centres to provide a clearer picture of the type of jobs available in the BBC. Links have been established with minority ethnic groups involved with media activities to encourage them to see the BBC as a potential employer.

With the BBC's move to its new White City premises, Hammersmith and Fulham, under Section 52 of the Town and Country Planning Act 1982, have asked that the organization should comply with 'Planning Gain'. This means that the BBC has to offer something back to the community as a recompense for disruption caused. The council agreed that the BBC should second a liaison officer to develop employment and training initiatives, eg a broadcast familiarization course. The final form of the initiative, however, will depend ultimately on what the residents want.

The results
Women in 1989 represent 56 per cent of the staff at junior managerial level and 15 per cent at Head of Department level.

A nursery for under-fives is to open early in 1990 and around 50 per cent of staff return to work after maternity leave. Job shares and part-time working are increasing and an extended career-break scheme has been introduced with the possibility of staff negotiating a five year break.

The Director-General chairs regular meetings on personnel strategy at which equal opportunities is a priority. The BBC's five year plan emphasized a commitment to 'continue to implement the EO Policy'.

The BBC is a good example of an organization which has fully endorsed a report, asked for by the Board of Governors and Board of Management, which recommended changes which have subsequently been implemented. As a next step the BBC is currently discussing internally the results of their ethnic monitoring exercise and how their activities should be focused in the 1990s.

The public sector: ILEA

The ILEA* is the local education authority for the twelve inner London Boroughs and the City of London. Education is provided in over 1,000 schools for over 280,000 pupils, and in 20 colleges and five polytechnics attended by over 225,000 full and part-time students. In addition, over 300,000 adults attend courses at the Authority's adult education institutes and aided establishments. They are taught by about 27,000 teachers and lecturers. In total, the ILEA employs over 90,000 members of staff. The ILEA is the only single purpose local education authority in the country and, as such, is in some ways not directly comparable with other education authorities.

The area served by the ILEA consists of 114 square miles and has a resident population of some 2.3m. The Education Service provides for those who work and study in inner London as well as for those who live there. As the largest local education authority in England, the Authority provides a wide range of facilities for all sections of the population in a densely populated multi-cultural inner city area.

Education in inner London has been provided by a unitary authority composed of elected members for over 100 years. From 1870–1904 there was the London School Board, which provided elementary education for all. From 1904–1965 education was the responsibility of the London County Council's Education Committee. The Inner London Education Authority, established in 1964,

now abolished

assumed their powers on the abolition of the LCC in 1965. After the abolition of the Greater London Council, direct elections were held in May 1986 for the new ILEA. Legislation has now been enacted to abolish the ILEA in April 1990 and to transfer education services to the inner London Borough Councils.

The policies to be pursued by the Authority are, as for other local authorities, decided by the elected members. The ILEA is composed of 58 member with two representatives for each of the 29 parliamentary constituencies in inner London. The present composition is Labour 45, Conservative 11, Social and Liberal Democrats 1, with one vacancy.

Policy statement
'The Authority is an equal opportunities employer. The aim of the policy is to ensure that no job applicant or employee receives less favourable treatment on grounds of sex, age, disability, race, colour, nationality, ethnic or national origins, marital status, being lesbian or gay, family responsibility, trade union activity, class, political or religious belief. Selection criteria and procedures will be kept under review to ensure that individuals are selected, promoted and treated on the basis of their relative merits and abilities. All employees will be given equal opportunity and, where appropriate, special training to progress within the organization. The Authority is committed to a programme of positive action to make this policy fully effective and to monitor progress.'

Aims of the policy
The policy aims to work within the legal context of the Race Relations Act 1976, The Equal Treatment Directive, The Sex Discrimination Act 1975, the Equal Pay Act 1970 and the Disabled Persons Acts 1944 and 1958. A great deal of the energy and impetus for the introduction of equal opportunities employment policies in ILEA came from the elected members.

History of equal opportunities
1 In April 1975 the ILEA issued a formal equal opportunities statement. This was expanded in 1982.

2 At this time an Equal Opportunities Unit and Equal Opportunities Advisory Group were set up, with trade union representation. Responsibility for promoting equal opportunities

was placed at the highest level of management in the Authority.

3 Between 1982–6 the main impetus towards establishing and achieving equal employment opportunities aims came from the GLC. The GLC adopted a wide range of often pioneering initiatives covering every aspect of the personnel process. Achievements included:

- a doubling in the proportions of minority ethnic staff

- major improvements in the levels of entry of women to senior posts

- the establishment of a comprehensive, computer-based equal opportunities monitoring scheme

- re-directing the bulk of established and new training budgets towards setting up Second Chance, Accelerated development, Access and Tester courses targeted specifically at previously excluded groups

- a complete overhaul of the GLC/ILEA grievance, discipline and career appraisal procedures, to ensure fair treatment

- regular consulation meetings with minority ethnic groups, women, disabled people and gay and lesbian staff

- the establishment of two 50-place GLC/ILEA staff day nurseries together with a major package of financial assistance for working parents

- establishing an equality target structure for all departments, linked to quarterly reviews based on the established personnel information data base.

4 In May 1985, the ILEA approved 'ILEA 5270', which proposed the introduction of a comprehensive scheme to monitor the composition of the ILEA workforce so that recruitment, promotion, training and career development plans could be directed towards redressing patterns of inequality. Despite strenuous efforts from members and officers, the ILEA survey was never fully completed, and this had a major inhibiting effect on its ability to develop a range of positive action measures similar to those which were implemented by the GLC.

It also meant that ILEA were not able to adopt equality targeting.

5   In April 1986, following the establishment of the new ILEA, an Equal Employment Opportunity Division was set up. This was established within the central unified personnel department in an attempt to overcome some of the structural barriers which had limited the effectiveness of attempts to follow through the Authority's Equal Opportunity Policy. What became clear in the early months of the 'new' Authority was that many of the GLC/ILEA policy decisions, eg opening up recruitment practices, financial assistance programmes for child care, had not in fact been applied within the ILEA.

6   A survey of the ethnic origin of 90,000 ILEA employees was carried out in January 1986. Following this, ethnic monitoring procedures on new recruits to the Authority were introduced.

Positive action within the policy

1   Closed entry systems to jobs
The GLC introduced an open grading system for white collar staff in 1983 which removed regulations restricting the class and grade of job which a member of staff could apply for. This opened up career opportunities for all GLC/ILEA staff and was particularly beneficial to those in the lower grades where most women and minority ethnic staff are employed.

2   Open recruitment
In moving towards open recruitment practices, word-of-mouth recruitment was eliminated; job specifications listed selection criteria, and procedures for recording shortlisting and appointment decisions according to these criteria were introduced.

3   Training
Training as a way of implementing the ILEA's commitment to equal opportunities has taken place in the following areas:

• selection interviewing courses for white collar staff

• governors' training

• specifically targeted training aimed at opening up opportunities for women, minority ethnic groups and people with disabilities. This has included:

courses in personal safety for women cleaners, started in 1988, run for women who work late at night or on their own in empty buildings

training in management skills, career planning and being interviewed, available in some instances specifically for minority ethnic staff

a new BTEC national diploma in caring services (nursery nursing) designed to be directly relevant to public sector work in an inner city, multi-cultural setting. This course is an entry qualification for BEd courses. Trainees represented include mature, bilingual and minority ethnic women.

work-related communication skills courses for manual workers, aimed at staff for whom training is difficult to organize because of unsocial hours, shift work and the need to provide cover,

in 1985–86 £112,000 was allocated to teachers' centres to provide courses to foster good practice in recruitment for heads, principals and others responsible for recruitment, and to provide support for career and professional development for teaching staff in groups under-represented at higher teaching levels eg women and minority ethnic teachers.

4   Parental support

Two 50-place workplace nurseries – one in County Hall and the other in Peckham – opened in 1984 following an agreement between the ILEA and GLC. Places were divided between the ILEA and GLC staff, and funded by the council and in part by charges paid by parents using the places. On the abolition of the GLC the two workplace nurseries were transferred to ILEA.

5   Job sharing

Job sharing is available to existing and potential employees within ILEA, with the exception of a small number of posts.

6 Grievance and discipline procedures
Grievance and discipline cases are closely monitored to identify patterns of problems which may need to be addressed by management action.

7 Monitoring
Following the introduction of monitoring procedures in 1986, the gathered information showed that only 1.4 per cent of the workforce was registered disabled. The Disabled Persons Act set a target of 3 per cent of an organization's workforce

8 Harmonization of terms and conditions of employment
Within the context of increasingly severe financial constraints, the Authority was able to make some progress between 1986–8 in reducing unnecessary and unfair differences in the contractual employment benefits available to different groups of staff. In general, this has involved rounding up the benefits of the lower paid to a level enjoyed by the higher paid staff.

Problems and outcomes
Progress towards the Authority's objectives has been slow and difficult. It is interesting to look at what problems were faced:

- lack of clarity on the scope of the policy meant that the need for accountability and consistent interpretation of policies was neglected and too much was left to the discretion of individual officers.

- the Equal Opportunities Unit was marginalized in organizational and management terms and under-resourced, and so found it difficult to achieve an authority-wide impact.

- the structure of the ILEA pre-1986 meant that equal opportunity policies could not be introduced as a series of building blocks. There was no central personnel presence so that only limited control could be exerted over recruitment, promotion, training etc. The organizational means of implementation, therefore, were not in place. This became particularly clear in the Authority's inability to implement member-agreed GLC/ILEA initiatives on equal opportunities.

- ILEA was decentralized into individual educational establishments to ensure a service tailored to local needs. Its influence was, however, limited where governors selected staff, particularly in voluntary schools. This meant that ILEA was accountable for staff it did not select, and that governing bodies carried out major personnel functions such as selection and grievance and discipline procedures.

- the scale of recruitment [8000 appointments between January 1986 and January 1987] together with dispersed personnel functions meant a massive resource and organizational problem in briefing and training staff and governors involved in recruitment. Financial restraints have meant that this training didn't take place.

- resources allocated to equal opportunities training have mainly been concentrated on changing managerial work practices. Little funding has therefore been available for publicity material which has meant little promotion of the benefits and responsibilities of equal opportunities, or for the range of qualifications-related positive action training programmes needed to launch black, female and disabled staff into work areas and grade levels where they had previously been excluded.

- lack of a monitoring system has meant that the ILEA cannot demonstrate the advantages of equal opportunities policies, nor find out their effects.

- all these factors, together with the size and diversity of the ILEA, means the Authority is substantially behind other inner city local authorities in terms of equal opportunities policies.

The private sector: Littlewoods

The Littlewoods organization consists of a mail order business, retail stores, a print company and a football pools business. It employs nearly 32,000 people; its employees are predominantly white and female.

Its head office is in Liverpool, where there are 2,500 members of staff. Most of these are white women in full-time jobs. Men carry out the senior jobs. Minority ethnic staff make up 2.6 per cent of the total there.

The football pools business, which is a separate company based in the North West, employs 5000 staff, most of whom are white women. Eight per cent of staff are from minority ethnic groups. This company used to have a 'mothers and daughters' recruitment policy which was formally brought to an end three years ago, although its effects continue.

The retail stores are based in all parts of the country and employ around 15,000 staff, who are mainly female except in management grades. The proportion of minority ethnic staff is 5.1 per cent.

The print company, J & C Moores, clearly distinguishes between male and female jobs; there are no minority ethnic staff. The print union recruits its own members.

Policy statement objectives

To ensure that the talents and resources of employees are utilized to the full and that no job applicant or employee receives less favourable treatment on the grounds of gender, marital status, social class, colour, race, ethnic origin, creed or disability or is disadvantaged by conditions or requirements which cannot be shown to be relevant to performance.

Littlewood's target is to ensure that there is a fair representation of minority ethnic people throughout the company by 1992. The meaning of 'fair representation' is one based on employing minority ethnic staff in direct proportion to their numbers in the local community. By 1992, therefore, there should be 8 per cent staff of minority ethnic origin at head office and in the stores and football pools sites in the North West.

History of equal opportunities policy

The commitment to equal opportunities practices emanates from John Moores, Littlewoods' chairman.

Up to the mid 1960s Littlewoods operated a policy of kinship recruitment. Complaints of how this resulted in religious discrimination occasioned an investigation which identified other forms of discrimination. An attempt to counter race discrimination led to a 'non-European' policy being adopted in 1967 with a 5 per cent target. This was not actively pursued. An equal opportunity policy was adopted in 1979 more as a protective response for the company against liability under the new sex and race discrimination laws than for moral reasons.

The Toxteth riots in 1981 once more focused attention on the need for active equal opportunities policies within Littlewoods. A code of practice was agreed in 1982, revised and updated in 1987. 1982 also saw the recruitment of relations advisor; an equal opportunities unit was established in 1986. Data on ethnic origin and gender are collected and monitored and a five-year programme for meeting targets has been established. Equality targets are built into appraisal systems, and the equal opportunity unit is working on a code of practice for recruitment and selection procedures.

Positive action

Recruitment practices
In the north, the emphasis in the practical implementation of these policies lies on recruitment.

Generally, jobs outside the retail stores are filled through internal advertising, which presents a barrier to recruiting minority ethnic groups and conflicts with Littlewood's own equal opportunity code of practice. This has proved very difficult to alter and the company has only recently changed its policy. The role of the unions has been ambivalent in this situation, and in essence they have inadvertently played a major role in maintaining the practice. During a big redundancy and redeployment programme in 1978 an internal advertising policy was agreed between unions and management, in which the unions' aim was to protect the rights of their existing membership rather than encourage the recruitment of minority ethnic staff.

The race relations officer at Littlewoods has organized seminars on race equality and equal opportunities for union officials and managers of the print company, which has no minority ethnic employees.

Promotion and flexible work hours
Other examples of positive action which Littlewoods have pursued include industrial language training for Asian employees in the Bolton area where the mail order sites are located. There was also an instance where a Muslim employee needed to take two hours off work each Friday to attend the local mosque where he had special responsibilities. At first his contract was changed,

which made his work effectively part-time; then the organization responded by enabling him to make up the hours at other times. Parallel requests were then made by four temporary Christmas workers; Littlewoods' decision not to make a similar arrangement, because they were only employed for six weeks, was upheld by the CRE.

Littlewoods is also involved in outreach work into the community including funding the Liverpool 8 Law Centre and South-Liverpool Personnel, an employment agency focussing on minority ethnic people, and involvement in a new local newspaper for minority ethnic people.

The focus of Littlewoods' equal opportunities policies lies on recruitment. They are aiming to offer equal entry into the workforce to bring their proportion of minority ethnic employees in line with the local population. This approach is inevitably starting to penetrate into their employment practices and procedures, to lead to equality of outcome in terms of career progression.

The private sector: Barclays Bank

Barclays Bank employs 87,000 people throughout the UK, including a sizeable number of part-time staff. The structure of the company operates on two bases – a regional and a departmental structure. Within this structure there is a central personnel function including an equal opportuniities manager, which is important for the introduction and operation of equal opportunity policies.

56,000 people work in 24 regions around the country. Each region has a centre which provides direction for its branches. The regions differ in size, and for instance in London there are seven because of the large number of customers. On average there are 2,300 members of staff in each region.

The management hierarchy in the regions is such that the personnel manager reports directly to the resources director who, in turn, reports to the regional director. It is the regional director who makes management decisions and ensures that central policy guidelines are adhered to. The personnel manager has responsibility for equal opportunities written into his or her job description.

There are a number of departments cutting across the hierarchical regional structure. These include the retail services division (incorporating Barclaycard), the central information systems department (with responsibility for service delivery utilizing information technology), financial services operation (insurance unit trusts etc. with an office in each regional centre) and a range of central departments such as the treasury division, marketing support, property services, catering etc. Each of these departments has a personnel function or administrative staff with personnel responsibility.

Centrally, the deputy director of personnel chairs the equal opportunities steering committee which includes the heads of other personnel sections covering career development, employee relations and training.

Policy statement

Equal opportunities – sex, race and marital status
The Bank is committed to providing equal opportunities in employment. This means that all job applicants and employees shall receive equal treatment regardless of sex, marital status, race, colour, nationality or ethnic or national origins.

Equal opportunities – disabled
The Bank recognizes that most people with disabilities have the same skills and abilities as other employees. It wishes to recruit and provide equal opportunities for disabled persons according to their abilities.

This statement is in the introduction of a Barclays Equal Opportunities booklet, which is a guide for staff working for Barclays Bank in the UK.

History of equal opportunities in Barclays
The stimulus for the introduction of equal opportunities policies within Barclays came from the Equal Opportunities Commission. The Commission's intervention followed a complaint from a school in 1983 that Barclays had interviewed a male applicant of 'A' level standard and had not offered an interview to a female applicant with similar qualifications from the same school.

The Equal Opportunities Commission proposed to conduct a formal investigation into recruitment policies within the Bank, but deferred this when Barclays agreed to introduce changes to meet the Commission's requirements.

The objectives of the agreement are to ensure that there are no practices or arrangements in the recruitment procedures now used by the Bank which contravene the Sex Discrimination Act.

The basic problem behind the Bank's recruitment policies was the assumption that men required a career and possessed managerial potential, and so the Bank's managers had apparently set higher educational qualifications for male recruits. It also appeared that girls were regarded as having only a short-term career within the Bank since as many as 90 per cent of all female recruits left within 15 years. Girls were therefore recruited with lower academic achievements to fill the large number of routine and clerical jobs in the Bank's branches.

Other parts of the agreement covered the implementation of new recruitment practices, the issuing of an equal opportunity policy document and training in sex discrimination legislation for recruiters.

This agreement was set for a four year period in which Barclays had to implement the Equal Opportunity Commission's recommendations.

Positive action within the policy

Following the Equal Opportunity Commission's agreement, Barclays have introduced the following positive action practices:

1   appointment of a Manager for Equal Opportunities who advises the Bank on the implementation and development of its policies and has responsibility for monitoring them. Personnel managers have specific responsibility for policy implementation;

2   a guide to the Bank's equal opportunities policies and its practices was issued to all staff in November 1985. All new recruits to the Bank receive a copy. This covers the equal opportunities policy statement, relevant legislation, and codes of practice, and a section on putting policies into practice. This section gives staff the setting in which their own company's equal opportunities policies have developed. The role of changes in legislation, the traditional family structure, the development of a multiracial society, demands for an increase in responsibility from minority ethnic groups and women, and demographic trends are all outlined. Positive action is not

something which is being imposed from above but is the responsiblity of each individual within the company. Existing assumptions are confronted by stating them clearly as beliefs which need to be challenged. For instance:

> people from minority ethnic groups lack the qualifications and skill for a banking career, or

> customers would not like a female or black bank manager;

3   there is close liaison over policies and action plans between the Bank and the EOC, CRE, Barclays Staff Union and the Banking, Insurance and Finance Union.' The Department of Employment's Service has been consulted on the employment of people with disabilities;

4   monitoring systems have been introduced to record statistics for all stages of the recruitment process to ensure equal treatment of all applicants, regardless of gender or race. There has also been an ethnic audit of the workforce;

5   the EOC's and CRE's Codes of Practice have been distributed throughout the personnel function in the Bank;

6   recruitment advertisements are placed in ethnic newspapers;

7   the Bank's pension arrangements have been adjusted to allow widowers to claim pension rights on the death of a married female member of staff or pensioner;

8   there is emphasis on the employment of people with disabilities and regular requests to meet the annual target of disabled recruits. There are also reminders concerning the special equipment and grants provided by the Employment Service to help disabled people;

9   there is a flexible career break scheme;

10   a booklet, *A Guide to Maternity at Work*, has been produced advising women of their legal rights to maternity pay and leave. Guidelines promoting flexibility in employing pregnant women and new mothers have been issued;

11   there have been revisions to the mobility clause in each member of staff's contract which reflect the degree of mobility

required to fulfil his/her career potential and meet the needs of the business.

Outcomes

The size and structure of Barclays has both positive and negative effects on the implementation of equal opportunity policies. Advantages include the fact that responsibility for the practice of the policy is clearly allocated; disadvantages occur with particular interpretation personnel managers may give to EO. Local environments tend to affect the enthusiasm with which the policies are utilized. For instance in areas where there is little unemployment, low demand for work from women and few minority ethnic people as a proportion of the population, the personnel manager may feel little impetus actively to introduce the policies.

Management attitude, therefore, has an important effect on implementation. Personnel managers are responsible for recruitment, but line managers involved in interviewing have to have had two days training in recruitment and selection in an equal opportunities context.

This approach forms a pattern for equal opportunity training within Barclays. Rather than being presented as a separate issue, it is integrated into other staff training activities, eg management skills training includes a session where managers discuss where their prejudices lie, and how to leave them behind when making decisions. Visual images are used as a way of stimulating this discussion.

A new approach is a course introduced in 1989 called *Managing People Fairly*. This covers EO legislation on gender, race and disability, looks at practically-based true/false situations, re-emphasizing the Bank's policy, and aims to develop a sense of personal liability for discriminatory actions. Again visual images are important, and a video has been made which challenges basic, easily-held assumptions, and raises issues which can develop into discussion topics.

This course is being run on a regional basis with participants from every appointed level. Barclays is aiming to involve 10,500 staff members in this course by the end of 1989.

As far as Barclays is concerned, EO has become an essential part of a good personnel practice and positively enhances systems which were previously in place.

Communication of the policy
The central equal opportunities manager visits the regions and departments regularly. An EO briefing in the form of a newsletter goes out regularly three times each year covering a wide range of issues and examples of good practice. Courses are also run centrally. The equal opportunities manager feels that the personal visits are the most effective way of keeping in touch and giving a clear direction to the policy.

Monitoring
The monitoring system has shown the effectiveness of the Bank's policies. As a response to these, Barclays is introducing targets to aim for in the recruitment of certain groups, eg during 1989 each recruitment point has to recruit three disabled people. Visually open employment is viewed as a very positive concept in terms of encouraging different members of that group to apply to the Bank.

Social responsibility
Barclays has a social responsibility budget which reflects the importance they attach to contributing towards a stable society. Projects sponsored from this budget have included a group developing disability training. Possibilities for the future include training for minority ethnic groups to open access to careers in banking.

Chapter 7   Education, training and employment

Starting equal: education

It is impossible to look at equality practices within a workforce without recognizing that people enter that workforce with different educational backgrounds and training experiences.

New initiatives in schools are beginning to build a bridge between education and work, not only for academically able children, but for other children as well. Where, however the perceptions and expectations that the child brings have been formed in an unequal educational environment, any action which employers take to make opportunities open to all will inevitably be too late.

The aim of this chapter is to define the main educational and training programmes with which employers will come in contact and to outline the main recommendations which have been made to try and ensure greater equality in people under the age of 18.

Inequalities in education

Inequality may take the form of boys being encouraged to take exclusively technically-based options. It may be shown through girls being misdirected in a different way. For instance: although girls perform better than boys in examinations at 16, where 14 per cent obtain five or more higher grade O Level and CSE passes compared with 11 per cent of boys, they are concentrated in the arts and domestic subjects, not in scientific, technical and technological subjects. The lack of qualifications in these subjects prevents young people from entering occupations ranging from physiotherapy, microbiology, air traffic control to photography and specifically new technologies where expansion continues to take place. Girls who have left school obtain a very small percentage of day release places to further their qualifications compared with boys of a similar educational standard. Careers counselling does not always make clear the importance of different combinations of examination subjects. This lack of counselling affects many boys equally badly, but the perception of maths, physical science and technology as 'subjects for boys' inevitably directs them into relevant and useful combinations of subjects.[1]

A more complex picture appears with minority ethnic children and their experience in the education system, and a committee of inquiry, chaired by Lord Swann, was established in 1979 to look at this area.

The Swann Report

In March 1985 the Committee of Inquiry into the Education of Children from Ethnic Minority Groups, presented its report. This report analyzed the position of West Indian children in the education system and made recommendations to improve it. It is worth looking at these recommendations in some detail to understand the problems of starting equal. The following statistics were drawn from 6 local education authorities (LEAs) in a DES school leavers survey, 1978/1979, covering approximately half of the school leavers from ethnic minority groups.

In all CSE and GCE 'O' level examinations only three per cent of West Indians obtained 5 or more higher grades (A–C) at 'O' level and Grade 1 CSE compared with 18 per cent of Asians and 16 per cent of all other leavers in those LEAs.

At GCE 'A' level only two per cent of West Indians gained one or more pass compared with 13 per cent of Asians and 12 per cent of all other leavers in these LEAs.

Only one per cent of West Indians went on to university compared with three per cent of Asians and three per cent of all other leavers in those LEAs.

Only one per cent of West Indians went on to full time degree courses in further education compared with five per cent of Asians and four per cent of all other leavers in these LEAs.

On the basis of this, the report stated the following:

> 'The Committee concludes that although there will
> "always be some children who will under-achieve and
> for various reasons will fail to reach their full potential"
> their concern is that West Indian children *as a group*

are "under-achieving in relation to their peers, not least in obtaining the examination qualifications needed to give them equality of opportunity in the employment market and to enable them to take advantage of the range of post-school opportunities available." [2]

The report looked at the factors which contributed to this under-achievement and the strategies needed to address it. Its conclusions are contained in Tables I and II.

Table I

Factors contributing to under-achievement of West Indian children (taken from the Swann Report):

- low teacher expectations of West Indian pupils' abilities and potential. Stereotypes, negative and patronizing views may provoke a self-fulfilling prophecy and can be seen as a form of 'unintentional racism'

- pre-school provision is inadequate to meet the needs of West Indian families. Local authorities should do more to ensure that parents are aware of the pre-school facilities available, and LEAs should do more to help parents appreciate the contribution they can make to the child's development before he or she starts school

- low attainment in reading by West Indian children could be alleviated by involving parents in helping their children learn to read

- a multi-cultural curriculum should be adopted by all schools to 'draw up on the experiences of the many cultures that make up our society and thus broaden the cultural horizons of every child'. Head teachers and teachers have a major part to play in this

- books and teaching materials should present a positive picture of minority ethnic groups and other cultures

- examination syllabuses need to become more relevant to the experiences of children in schools today

- in terms of pastoral care, LEAs should provide in-service courses on the particular needs of minority ethnic pupils

- 'the gulf in trust and understanding between schools and West

Indian parents needs to be breached'. Schools should 'reach out' to parents, eg through more teachers undertaking home visiting. The West Indian community are encouraged to seek ways of actively being involved in the school's work

● no ethnically-based statistics are available to monitor how many West Indian children were placed wrongly in schools catering for special needs. The report recommends a variety of measures concerning referral to these units, and recommends that ethnically-based statistics should be collected, and urges LEAs to 'take full account of the particular factors, such as cultural differences and the effects of discrimination, which may have a bearing on the educational progress of West Indian children.'

Table II

Strategies for action (taken from the Swann Report):

● head teachers and teachers should take a key role in making the education system more responsive to the needs of minority ethnic children

● initial teacher training has provided little guidance or grounding in multi-cultural education and all teacher-training institutions need to review their policies in this respect

● schools should establish effective induction programmes for teachers

● in-service training should encourage a multi-cultural approach

● there should be more West Indian teachers and professionals at all levels in the education service and more 'special access' courses into teacher training for minority ethnic people. [For instance, only two per cent of teachers came from minority ethnic groups although such groups now account for 4.5 per cent of the population. More than 75 per cent of black and Asian teachers were on the bottom two teaching grades compared to 57 per cent of white teachers (CRE report)]. In areas with substantial minority ethnic populations, LEAs should appoint a multi-cultural advizer with 'a genuine understanding of minority ethnic pupils and a knowledge of the minority communities' cultures and concerns'.

● a range of ethnically-based statistics should be gathered from 1 September 1982

The findings of the Swann Report have been the cause of some controversy, but its recommendations stimulated government to introduce a voluntary ethnic monitoring system into all LEA and grant-maintained schools from September 1990.

Employers' needs
What are employers looking for when they recruit 16–18 year olds? It is difficult to generalize, but it seems they are looking for a sound, all-round education. They are also increasingly in favour of the schemes being developed in schools where pupils gain experience of the work environment as part of their learning. It is worth looking at the main schemes for this age group to see how they correspond with the needs of employers.

GCSE
In June 1984, the government announced a single system of examinations at 16+ – the GCSE – which would replace 'O' level, CSE and other 16+ exams in England and Wales from the summer of 1988. Syllabuses, assessment and grading procedures are based on national criteria, established by DES. Ongoing assessment, over two years, is based on coursework alone or combined with examinations to give final results. This method of assessment of their work and progress is likely to be more detailed and helpful for employers and for colleges.

CPVE
In 1985 the Certificate of Pre-Vocational Education was introduced for school-leavers in England, Wales and Northern Ireland who have not yet decided which career or further education course they want to follow.

It is aimed at 16–17 year olds, and enables them to study a range of subjects and topics as a 'pre-entry' course prior to going into a job, with or without further education, to continue in full-time education, or go on to a vocational course leading to a City and Guilds or BTEC qualification.

Both educationalists and employers have design input into CPVE courses. Employers find that CPVE students are more mature and aware of their needs and potential. During CPVE they have a period of work experience which provides a realistic view of what is needed in a job. Assessment methods (including profiles) also help an employer by giving detailed evidence of what students can or cannot do.

A pilot project is presently under way to incorporate CPVE into the two-year YTS programme. This enables young people to get a broad-based nationally-recognized qualification before going on to job-specific experience and training within the second year of YTS.

BTEC
The City and Guilds of London Institute approves courses leading to the awards of the Institute which give commercial and industrial qualifications. These are highly thought of by employers as a firm basis for work skills.

TVEI
The Technical and Vocational Education Initiative is aimed at 14–18 year olds and offers work-linked, practical courses with strong industrial and commercial connections. The MSC launched TVEI in 1982 and by 1987 85 per cent of LEAs in England, Wales and Scotland had taken part.

It is organized through projects that involve technical skills, using machines, learning about computers, designing and making things. It is also vocational in that the projects are closely related to real jobs, and are designed to give experience of technical work, careers and courses. For instance, it will try and address the change in the structure of employment away from manual occupations towards higher-level information technology. TVEI aims to inform young people about computer technology and give them skills that can be added to as they move through employment.

An important part of TVEI is its work experience, where pupils go out to companies both to observe adults working and to work themselves. When it is not possible to spend several weeks with employers, visits, work observations or simulations are used.

YTS
The Youth Training Scheme was introduced in April 1983 to give everyone leaving school at 16 a year's planned work experience and training.

The aim of the YTS is to produce better-qualified entrants to the labour market and to give young people the skills, knowledge and experience which employers require.

Against a background of rising youth unemployment in the mid

1980s (in 1987, 1 in 5 of all those under 25 were unemployed) there has been a move towards everyone at 16 or 17 being in school, college or full-time training before taking their first job at 18. In April 1986, the YTS was extended to two years for 16 year olds with 20 weeks off-the-job training, and one year for 17 year olds with 7 weeks off-the-job training.

The YTS is organized by managing agents – employers, local authorities, voluntary organizations etc – who are responsible for all aspects of the training programme.

Over a million young people have gone through YTS and two-thirds have found a positive outcome – either jobs, further education or further training. Yet the existence of these schemes by themselves is not going to ensure that pupils have equal access to the programmes and thus a wide range of job opportunities. Nor will they ensure that employers can choose from enough or the right kind of school leavers. Nor will they ensure that discrimination at the intersection of education and employment disappears.

The CRE report, *Half a Chance* (1980), tested more than 100 firms in Nottingham. In over 50 per cent of cases, white job applicants were selected in preference to equally qualified black applicants. In over one third of the cases, two black applicants were rejected in favour of the white applicant.

An awareness of this has led to clearly stated equal opportunities policies, particularly in TVEI and YTS.

TVEI and equal opportunities
Under the terms of TVEI each participating local education authority has to satisfy a number of criteria. The first of these criteria states that:

> girls and boys should normally be taught together and care should be taken to avoid discrimination and sex stereotyping.

This emphasis on equal opportunities seems to have had a positive effect on the operation of the programme. For instance five out of 11 Fawcett Society awards for positive action went to TVEI schools in recognition of their work in encouraging girls to move into non-traditional areas of the curriculum. In TVEI, the percentage of girls taking technology subjects has risen to 2.23 per cent from 0.3 per cent prior to TVEI; for Information Technology the figures are 13 per cent and 2.39 per cent. The increase in the percentage of girls in TVEI taking these subjects is higher than the increase in the percentage of boys.[3]

TVEI and parents
It is important, in a well-funded TVEI scheme, that parents understand the scope of TVEI, its aims and general ethos, and are involved in its development. Schools should make clear to parents the educational justification for the equal opportunities aspect of TVEI and thereby help them to overcome any resistance to their daughter or son's choice of a non-traditional career. It is also important to emphasize the link with employment which TVEI offers: there is evidence that parents of minority ethnic students may be boycotting TVEI because they feel it has a non-academic, and therefore 'inferior' ethos. Yet the effectiveness of well-funded TVEI schemes as an entry into employment and as an introduction to a range of skills which can be applied in a variety of work situations is well-documented.

A report by Professor John Eggleson and Ms Edna Sadler of the Education Department of Warwick University, based on an examination of TVEI in a small number of West Midlands schools, found that many minority ethnic parents were inadequately informed about the status of the initiative. They considered it inferior to other courses and worried that their children would not be able to aspire to professional and white-collar careers if they followed a TVEI programme.

This perception was reinforced by the nature of the work experience forming part of TVEI which often consisted of brief spells in low status manual or service jobs. Among the study's recommendations are for more face to face communication between schools and parents about TVEI to overcome language barriers in Asian families.

TVEI and employers
The importance of employer participation in the scheme cannot be overemphasized from an equal opportunities viewpoint. This should take one or all of the following approaches:

• participation in the planning of the TVEI programme

• active recruitment of students into non-traditional areas

- to ensure, with schools, access to the full range of skills areas through work placement for minority ethnic students

- non-specification of the gender or ethnicity of the applicant when recruiting students to work experience programmes

- science and industry should offer the services of employees working in non-traditional occupations as visitors and speakers to schools, and invite groups of students to visit factories and workshops before they opt for work experience, and should encourage minority ethnic students by ensuring that visitors from the industry are representative of minority ethnic communities

- participation in open evenings for TVEI students, parents and teachers.

YTS and equal opportunities
1986–87 was the first year of operation of the two year YTS. The Youth Training Board undertook regular reviews of the progress being made on equal opportunities. Structural changes were made to the programme at this point, including:

- a positive commitment to equal opportunities as one of the 10 criteria tested for the award of Approved Training Organisation status

- strengthening of the equal opportunities section of the YTS contract between the Training Agency and the managing agent

- the need for managing agents to state in training proposals practical steps which they have taken towards implementing equal opportunities

- a programme of compulsory training in equal opportunities for all field staff involved in the delivery of YTS

- increase in number of YTS development offices from 20 to 30 to promote YTS within minority communities

- YTS marketing literature designed to promote equal opportunities and avoid stereotyped images

- special assessment courses, adaptations to the equipment, and permanent additional funding for the disabled were measures designed to enable young people with disabilities to participate in YTS.

However, despite clearly-stated objectives, the operation of YTS has been open to criticism on equal opportunities.

An article in the November issue of *Training Tomorrow* suggests that minority ethnic school leavers are not being recruited onto the most prestigious YTS schemes. These schemes, run by well-known high street stores, manufacturers and financial institutions offer good conditions for trainees including top-ups to the allowance, high job success rates and training programmes linked to apprenticeships. The report, *The Firms that like to Say No*[4] stated:

'The existence of such high levels of racial inequality on YTS has been fuelled by a combination of ignorance, indifference and hostility from the Training Commission, YTS Managing Agencies and the Careers Service towards the implementation of equal opportunity polices.'

It went on to emphasize the need for the Training Agency to withdraw training grants from firms which don't recruit minority ethnic trainees and points out that the prospect of compulsory YTS for unemployed school leavers will make things even worse.

Compacts
The government announced in March 1988 that it was providing £12 million over the next four years to develop industry/education 'compacts' around the country, principally in inner-city areas.

Compacts are joint initiatives by businesses and the local education authority and aim to support the work of schools, provide firm job prospects for students who meet agreed standards, and generally raise levels of achievement.

London Education Business Partnership
One compact, the LEBP, is already running in East London, the idea of LENTA (a non-political organization of 17 major national employers) and ILEA. A joint group of employers and head teachers carry responsibility and four schools in Hackney and Tower Hamlets are involved.

The companies currently in the compact are involved in retailing, communication, computers, word-processing, oil products, hotel/catering, electrical work, telecommunications, electronics, insurance, banking and accountancy. These member companies have accepted a target of 300 jobs to be provided for fifth year leavers from these schools in June/July 1988. They have also accepted further goals to provide schools with the infrastructure, support and continuous involvement which will enable them to meet the expectations of the business world.

Equally the students are given targets, involving good attendance, punctuality, completion of courses and work experience. They are also encouraged to move into further education, if suitable, and they all take part in a community service project. Equal opportunities are an integral part of the goals established for the participants.

It is early days yet to draw any conclusions about the operation of the compact. It is becoming clear that it needs to steer a middle course to ensure that the students have access to jobs which suit them and which provide interest and career progression.

The Careers Service

The role of the careers service is vital in ensuring a bridge between school and employment which offers equality to all school leavers, regardless of gender, ethnicity or disability.

The CRE suggested that the careers service needs a clear statement of equal opportunity objectives, and a system which monitors progress in achieving these aims. The resulting information would need to be systematically reviewed and used as a basis for future action. This would show the service the impact of its own policies, would identify any potential in-house discrimination, and target work with employers, colleges and training managers who appear to be acting in a discriminatory manner.

However, although the careers service can monitor opportunities and outcomes up to the age of 16 fairly easily, the monitoring of later employment moves may be dependent both on the willingness of organizations, institutions and companies to co-operate in the compilation of the data, and upon a joint commitment to act on it.

Higher education

Despite the introduction of the polytechnics in the 1970s, higher education is still the preserve of a small elite, who tend to be white and middle class.

Speaking at a recent conference[5], Tessa Blackstone, Master of Birkbeck College, proposed that there should be a shift in the direction of older, mature students entering higher education; a reversion of the scenario where full-time students are paid for by the local authority while part-time students have to pay their fees out of their own pockets; a review of entrance requirements away from academic qualifications towards relevant experience; an expansion of well-resourced access courses; increased outreach into the community and an expansion in post-experience vocational education, eg short courses in marketing or personnel.

Post-university

There is evidence that discrimination of post-graduates in terms of level and types of jobs gained operates widely.

In 1987, a CNAA Development Services Project at Bulmershe College of Higher Education, sponsored by CRE, carried out a study into the employment of graduates from minority ethnic groups.

This concluded that:

• graduates from minority ethnic groups appear to experience greater difficulties than UK Europeans in obtaining employment. A greater proportion is unemployed 12 months after graduation. The graduates themselves perceive greater difficulties in gaining employment than do their white counterparts

• the jobs gained by minority ethnic graduates appear to be inferior to the jobs gained by other graduates

• Asian graduates tended to have taken courses with very clear vocational outlets, but the employment profile tended to be different to other graduates, eg pharmacy – the Asian graduates entered more small firms in the private sector

• the number of Afro-Caribbean graduates was small and they were spread over a wider range of courses and types of employment than the Asian graduates. The data suggests, however, that these graduates were more successful in the labour market than the Asians

- educational qualifications do not eradicate inequalities grounded in gender or in ethnic origin.

Continuing equal: training

Who gets it?
People under 25 are most likely to have received training. In general, the incidence and amount of training declines steadily with age: in 1987 55 per cent of 19–24 year olds received training in the preceding three years, in comparison with 14 per cent of 55–59 year olds.

The amount of training received is higher for those on higher incomes. Those with low incomes (especially below £6,000 p.a.) received lower amounts of training than those with higher incomes.[6]

About one-third of working adults said they have never received any training during their working lives.

Employers and training
Employers cite the need to sharpen competitiveness as their main reason for providing training, and firms facing international competition tend to train more than other employers.

36 per cent of employers who trained said that they had found skill supply problems over the previous twelve months. Faced with these problems employers had responded in one or more ways, including: 25 per cent – no remedial action, 33 per cent – increased recruitment of skilled staff, 51 per cent – training of existing staff.[7]

Only 1/3 of employers have any training plan. Only 10 per cent undertake formal training needs analysis. Only 3 per cent of employers who train compared the benefits of the training provided, with the loss incurred. In a similar way to the tailoring of the education system to take cognisance of employers' needs, so too the training scene is moving closer to specific, vocationally related, employer-based programmes. This has wide implications for the infrastructure of training within which employers will work and its process, and for ensuring equality of access to, and outcomes from, that training.

NCVQ

The National Council for Vocational Qualifications was established in 1987 to develop a nationally-recognized network of qualifications closely allied to the needs of employers.

NCVQ was needed because of the variety of accrediting systems which are awarded at almost every level and in every field, and which represented a bewildering plethora of qualifications to potential employers. Some of these were valuable to employers; others applied standards which were out of touch with the real needs of work; some emphasized theory at the expense of practice; and while some occupations have many overlapping qualifications, others have none at all. This means employers can't tell how well-qualified job applicants really are; and employees can't tell which qualifications are going to be most appropriate to establishing or improving skills.

The aims of NCVQ are:

- to make the qualification system relevant to the needs of business and industry

- to make sure each occupation has its own clear set of qualifications

- to make the system effective and used by employers.

In establishing the new system NCVQ consults both employer and employee organizations to establish a standard of work that qualifications need to meet. When it meets the required standard it becomes an NCVQ qualification.

The NVQ system itself will become the national record of competence by the 1990s. Before then, a credit-accumulation system will be built, based on units of competence which can be achieved, recorded and then recognized by all awarding bodies as a credit toward a NVQ.

Each unit will be achieved through a variety of methods including courses, private study, open learning and learning at work. The new system will enable students to build up qualifications on a modular basis ie they will take courses which lead to all or part of a particular qualification and will be able to 'stagger' these courses throughout their working life. This will mean, for instance, that women with children will be able to study through the Open University and Open College, using distance learning techniques, and achieve national qualifications which will be relevant when they re-enter the workforce.

The Employment Training Managers' Handbook[8] states

> 'Eventually, all training should be aimed at these definitions of competencies and the skills associated with them. The system will also take account of any previous learning. Again it is also recommended that staff should maintain a Record of Achievement based upon these units and elements of competence.'

Employment Department Training Agency
(was Training Commission and Manpower Services Commission)

The Manpower Services Commission (MSC) was set up in 1973 by the Conservative Government's Employment and Training Act with a brief to 'help people train for and obtain jobs which satisfy their aspirations and abilities and to help employers find suitable workers'.

The first programme to be set up was the Youth Opportunities Programme (YOP) in 1978. This was replaced in 1983 by the Youth Training Scheme (YTS). Information Technology Centres (ITECs) offer training in information technology to young people aged 16 to 19 and the local community. They developed as part of YOP and YTS with funding from the MSC and Department of Trade and Industry (DTI). All adult training programmes, including the Community Programme and the Job Training Scheme were subsumed in 1988 into 'Employment Training', which is now the prime vehicle for adult training in Britain. During 1988, the name of the MSC was changed first to Training Commission, then to Employment Department Training Agency.

In the operation of its training programmes the Training Agency gives a firm commitment to equal opportunities. 'In terms of access to, participation in and benefit derived from its programmes by all regardless of their race, religion, sex, marital status or disability'.[9]

Employment Training

Employment Training, introduced on September 5, 1988 and so very much in its infancy, is a scheme which is aiming to bring the unemployed into the labour market by training them in and for skills which are in short supply. It is funded through a combination of government and private sector money. It aims to train 600,000 participants with a total Training Agency budget of £1.4bn.

Evidence is as yet slight on the success of Employment Training in giving equal access to training for all groups. The Training Agency aims to move towards Approved Training Organization (ATO) status by March 1990 for all providers and one of the measurements for this will be equal opportunities category.

Eligibility for the scheme mainly focusses on having been unemployed for six months. There are special exemptions to this, however, eg women returning to work. There is also a childcare allowance of up to £50 per week for single parents with school age children using a registered childminder.

Employment Training functions on the basis of a partnership between employer and training. Training is organized by training managers, and during work placement the employer pays an amount varying between £5.00 and £8.00 per day to the training manager responsible for the trainee. Training may be delivered:

1   by a training organization, which may be voluntary or a private training provider, in conjunction with a work placement on the employer's premises

2   by the employer.

All the training will lead eventually to NCVQ-recognized qualifications.

Employment Training was devised to provide employers with a clear focus on adult training, and to reach the long-term unemployed. Its advantages to employers should be that it gives access to sections of the workforce which were difficult to reach; that the trainees have previously been 'sifted' via consultation so that they are aiming for an occupational area which they, themselves want; that government and employer are sharing the cost of training; and that training will be directly tailored to the needs of industry.

Training and Enterprise Councils
The Government White Paper *Employment for the 1990s*[10] proposed a further consolidation of the link between training and employers with a plan to establish around 100 employer-led local Training and Enterprise Councils [TECs] over the next four years.

The role of TECs will be to draw up local training strategies, arrange for the delivery of suitable training programmes – in particular in providing support for small businesses – aimed at young people, the unemployed and workers made redundant or changing job, and to promote training within companies and establish close links with the education service. They will tailor national programmes such as YTS and Employment Training to local circumstances to meet particular skill needs.

They will be allocated between £15m and £50m a year and will be supported by local Training Agency staff. Although they will be employer-led, they will involve a wide range of people from the education service, the voluntary sector, the unions, and local authorities.

TECs are closely modelled on private industry councils in the US which were introduced in 1983. A national launch of the first TECs took place in Spring 1990.

Open University

The Open University offers university-level courses on a national basis which can be studied for and gained through open and distance learning techniques. These courses are not vocationally based.

Open learning techniques offer an increased flexibility in studying. The Open University system consists of a combination of learning techniques including:

- distance learning study
- group work and locally based groups working with an assigned tutor
- residential courses
- audio-visual materials
- text-based work and assignments.

Where techniques like these are combined with staggered access, so that individuals can join and leave programmes according to individual need, then barriers to learning which have traditionally existed for people with other commitments, including working parents, those with other dependents and, indeed, employees at work, are removed.

Open College

The Open College came into being in September 1987. Its aim is to enable individuals to update existing skills or learn new ones. It uses television broadcasts, distance training techniques and student support systems as a way of doing this. It aims its services both at employers, with special training packages for their employees, and individuals, who may pay for courses themselves.

The Open College, along with the Open University, uses open learning and distance learning techniques to impart skills. It is closely linked with the National Council for Vocational Qualifications, and each course which the Open College runs will eventually lead to a nationally recognized qualification. A network of gateway centres throughout the country offers tutorial support to participants. Television similarly offers a stimulus and support.

Because of the flexible nature of study, the Open College offers the opportunity for groups normally excluded from more conventional training to build up a series of qualifications which could lead towards employment. Its disadvantages are that it costs money and there is no state funding currently in operation to open access up to all who could potentially be involved.

The Open College is addressing certain of its courses to the issue of returning to work after a break. Current offerings include *Women, the Way Ahead*.

Other adult training initiatives

PICKUP

PICKUP stands for Professional, Industrial and Commercial Updating. The programme was launched by the DES in 1982. It covers England and Wales, and in Scotland there is now an allied programme of PICKUP Partnership Projects.

PICKUP aims to help colleges, polytechnics and universities to increase and improve the work they do in meeting the adult training, updating and retraining needs of employers and their workforces. It aims are to:

- tackle the financial and administrative disincentives to PICKUP so that employers meet with a quick, flexible and cost-effective response

- encourage new learning methods and approaches to the planning of training and updating activities

- increase awareness, particularly among employers, of the crucial need to invest in adult training.

The type of training in which PICKUP is involved is:

- vocational
- for those in employment
- post-experience (rather than initial training)
- collaborative, between colleges and employers
- short, part-time, cost-effective and flexible
- self-financing (the customer/consumer pays)

The training encompasses:

- short courses, tailor-made training packages for individuals, sites or whole organizations
- action learning
- independent study (programmes of open or distance learning)
- in-house training, bringing learning to the shop floor or office
- consultancy, research and support services.

Local Collaborative Projects
Funded by the Training Agency under the PICKUP programme to identify and match local skills and training provision.

CALLMI
Computer Assisted Local Labour Market Intelligence database, funded by the Training Agency. This requires regular surveys of companies to expand and update information.

TAPS
Training Access Points are being set up in a variety of locations including job centres, public libraries, high street shops and training organizations, to give information on training provision available to individuals and to business.

Local Employer Networks
A local employer network is a project aimed at increasing employer involvement in the planning and delivery of vocational education and training for the job. They were set up in 1987 through collaboration between the Training Agency, the CBI and the Association of British Chambers of Commerce.

The main functions of a network are:

* to collect and analyze relevant labour market information, feeding it both into local planning of vocational and training provision and back to employers

* to consult employers (large and small) about their requirements and represent them in the planning of local vocational training

* to provide a local source of advice and consultancy.

Further education colleges
Further education colleges are one of the main deliverers of education and training in the UK, with a wide range of vocationally-based courses tied into national accreditation systems.

In general, women are outnumbered in advanced further education courses while predominating in non-advanced and evening courses. Although the number of women students in higher education is increasing, they are underrepresented in subjects such as science, engineering and technology.

There is still a dominant attitude that post-school education should be undertaken between 16 and 21 years of age. The demand for continuing education is growing, particularly from mature women, but there is still inadequate provision of suitable opportunities. Nevertheless, further education colleges can provide a route into higher education for all those who do not follow the traditional route through to the school sixth form.[11]

Access courses
The majority of these courses are full-time; they normally attract a mandatory award. They are specifically for students without orthodox qualifications, eg mature students without standard academic qualifications, who may be regarded as acceptable to follow a course if they can satisfy the college of their ability to sustain

and successfully complete the course. Very often, experience is an important criterion in selection.

On 2 August 1987 the DES invited 7 LEAs to establish pilot special access courses for people whose existing needs had not been met by the existing statutory provision. Special emphasis was given in these to members of minority ethnic groups.

Special access courses are a form of 'positive action' lawful under section 35 of the Race Relations Act 1976. The object of positive action is to accelerate the progress of minority ethnic groups towards an equal distribution of the opportunities in society. Section 35 exempts:

> 'Any act done in affording persons of a particular racial group access to facilities or services to meet the special needs of persons of the groups in relation to their education, training or welfare, or any ancillary benefits.'

Despite this, little advantage has been taken of the opportunity for positive action afforded by section 35.

Return to work training

Courses for women returning to work are now available to ease the process and enable regaining of skills to take place.

Ideally, they include elements of confidence building, career planning and self-evaluation. First of all there is an introductory skills taster period following which the women choose the skill area they want to train in. They may undertake longer term training leading to nationally-recognized qualifications and to employment.

The role of the unions

In the past, the unions have placed a priority on negotiating pay settlements rather than pushing for training or the implementation of equal opportunities policies for their membership.

However, the TUC's paper *Skills for Success*[12] clearly backs vocationally-based education and training initiatives, and the MSF (Manufacturing, Science and Finance Union), have made moves to establish a clearly-defined policy on training as a part of employment rights. This will have a fundamental impact on opening up access and opportunities for previously neglected groups. It is worth taking a closer look at the MSF's policy[13] to see its implications. Its main aims are that:

1   details of access to training and re-training should be a fundamental part of an employee's contract of employment

2   clause 1 (3) of part one of the Employment Protection (Consolidation) Act 1978 should be amended, so that the length and nature of induction training and further details of all company retraining schemes to which the employee may be entitled are included in the written terms of employment.

Jointly negotiated training or staff development agreements between management and unions should contain the following principles:

• confirmation that each employee has the right to training and retraining after a minimum period of service

• the establishment of a joint company/union training committee to assess skill shortages and potential areas of redundancy and to determine training programmes with agreed and published budgets

• jointly agreed unbiased methods of aptitude testing to be provided by the company where appropriate

• regular individual career planning and counselling

• union representatives to be able to attend courses on employment trends and technology

• equal opportunities to be given priority at all levels of staff planning

• regular bulletins on staff planning and technology to be made available to all employees by the training committee.

References

1   JAMIESON, Alan, ed. *Which subject? Which career?*. London, Which? Books, Consumers' Association, 1988.
2   Committee of Inquiry into the Education of Children from Ethnic Minority Groups. 'Education for all'. London, HMSO, 1985.
3   EQUAL OPPORTUNITIES COMMISSION. 'Equal opportunities in TVEI', 1985.
4   TRAINING AGENCY, Youth Employment and Training Resource Unit. 'The firms that like to say no'. 1988.
5   BLACKSTONE, Tessa. 'Business development: a serious option for the black community?'. Presented at a Fullemploy conference, London, November 1988.
6   POLICY STUDIES INSTITUTE. Study on individual adult's training experience. 1987.
7   TRAINING AGENCY. 'The funding of vocational education and training: some early research findings'. Background note No. 2. 1988.
8   TRAINING AGENCY. *Employment training managers' handbook*. 1988.
9   HMSO, White Paper; 'Employment for the 1990s'. London, HMSO, 1988
10 *Ibid.*
11 DEPARTMENT OF EDUCATION AND SCIENCE, Further Education Unit. *Changing the focus: women and further education*. London, HMSO, 1985.
12 TRADES UNION CONGRESS: 'Skills for success'. London, TUC, 1989.
13 MANUFACTURING, SCIENCE AND SCIENCE UNION. Statement on equal opportunities in training, 1988.

Chapter 8 Future gazing

Equal employment policies are still, often, not being put into practice, which means that to project into the future is doubly difficult. The development of equal opportunities practices is so much part and parcel of wider movements in society, some of which are predictable and some of which happen at random, that trying to predict the shape of the next 20, 50 or 100 years becomes sheer speculation.

For instance, what will employment patterns look like in 50 years time? What impact will changes in technology make? What will the role of personnel be?

Some future gazing is more predictable. The effect of continued demographic change and skill shortages, equal opportunities and the single European market, the developing or waning influence of US anti-discrimination legislation on the UK and the long-term plans of the EOC and CRE in maintaining equal opportunities practices are all, to some extent, being established at the moment.

Before looking at the future, however, it is worth taking stock of the present pattern. Equal opportunities policies are not easy for employers to introduce and implement in the short term. They need understanding, commitment and long-term planning.

A report by the Institute of Manpower Studies[1] looked at 20 organizations who have introduced equal opportunity policies. Its results corresponded closely with the introductory process suggested in this book, stressing the need for backing from senior management, policies integrated into other personnel practices and clear communication channels. The majority of organizations concentrated on women or minority ethnic groups and introduced training initiatives as a first step, followed by policies aimed at the recruitment and selection process, and then policies concerned with promotion and career development. Interestingly, training and promotion activities were more commonly aimed at women, while recruitment initiatives focused on minority ethnic communities.

A second survey covering 21 of the leading 60 UK companies found that nearly all had an equal opportunities policy, monitored it and kept statistics on their workforce. Other initiatives, however, were aimed mainly at women and included training schemes specifically for women, 27 per cent with job-share schemes, seven per cent making payments towards childcare and none with nursery provision[2]. If this is today's pattern, what of the future?

Demographic changes and skill shortages

During the 1980s, skill shortages have surfaced in sharper profile with the fall in the number of young people coming on to the labour market. This projected fall, a decline of 27 per cent in 1993 compared with 1987[3], is linked with DES predictions that full-time education participation is essential if employers' longer-term needs for more highly qualified people are to be met. In the short-term, however, this will only add to recruitment difficulties.

The Autumn 1988 Quarterly Survey of Small Businesses includes examples of skills shortages, such as 18 per cent of respondents saying that lack of skilled employees was one of the most important problems they faced; an increase in respondents reporting difficulties in recruiting bricklayers and carpenters, 92 per cent of firms reporting skills shortages in the South, London and the Midlands and over 83 per cent of firms reporting shortages of plasterers in the same areas.[4]

Planning by employers is essential to meet future skill requirements. In planning ahead, a few large employers are expecting to take a significant share of the available young people. For example, at present, fewer than 20 large employers account for more than half of the available 'A' level recruits. There is already competition amongst employers and demand is expected to increase against the background of declining numbers available for employment.

On current health authority recruitment targets, nursing would need to take about 50 per cent of all females with good GCSE qualifications entering employment in England in 1995. Other areas recruiting school leavers at this level are technician traineeships, banking, building societies, the police, junior scientific support jobs and some types of clerical work such as the Civil Service and local authorities. The NHS and Civil Service are looking for other sources of recruits.

In view of the projected skill shortages, the Training Agency backed a four-point strategy for employers in April 1988. To meet future requirements, employers need to:

- provide structured training for young people when they start work

- recruit and train the adult unemployed including the disabled and minority ethnic groups for the available jobs

- recruit and train the adults who want to return to the labour market or who are not fully using their skills at the moment

- train and develop their own workforces to meet demand for skilled, experienced employees.

Against this background and the lack of realization by many employers of the scale of the skill shortage problem, it is worth looking at examples of sectors who have already planned or made moves to ensure sufficient employees by recruitment drives into new areas, by training courses or by more equal employment practices.

The Health Service

The Royal College of Nursing recommends:

- a job-share scheme so that when a group of students complete training at the same time, they will be able to share available jobs if there aren't enough initial vacancies. It is hoped that this will reduce the number of newly-qualified staff having to look for other types of work or training

- the introduction of flexible working hours to allow hospital staff to judge staffing levels on a day-to-day basis based on workload and also relate hours to domestic circumstances

- recruitment of more men and mature people. Of the 60,000 nurses who were training in 1986, less than 10,000 were over the age of 26. The number of men as a proportion of the whole is very small.

The Police Force

Police cadets, one source of recruits for Scotland Yard, no longer need the five GCSE exams required for entrance, but can opt to take an entrance exam instead. This is in direct response to demographic changes. 'There aren't enough youngsters to go around and we want the best ones we can get. We have found that some minority ethnic youngsters are at a disadvantage if English is not their first language. They may find it difficult at school, but that doesn't necessarily matter to us. We're looking for people with common sense. After all, we learn a lot of things at school we don't need in later life.'[5]

The figures which have precipitated this move are that in March 1989 there were 403 uniformed and 27 CID officers from minority ethnic groups in the Metropolitan police force out of a total of 28,120. 89 of the minority officers were women.

Maths teachers

13 per cent of maths teaching in secondary schools in 1984 was provided by teachers with no recorded qualification in the subject because of a shortage of maths-trained teachers. Trainee maths teachers who did not look for a teaching job gave as their reason poor salary, poor work conditions and low status.

Recommendations in a joint report issued by the Royal Society and the Institute of Mathematics and its Applications include:

- access to initial training needs to be made more flexible so that capable candidates are not prevented from entering training

- more support should be given to professional development for maths teachers, eg through OU courses

- changes in school maths should include curricula more relevant to the real world; 'A' levels could be cut back in content without loss of rigour or depth.

Engineering and new technology

Engineering currently employs more professional engineers, scientists and technicians but fewer craftsmen and unskilled workers than ever before. A result of this occupational shift is that half of all professional engineers in the engineering industry are new graduates.

Employers in the engineering industry who experienced recruitment difficulties took the following action:

- developed closer links with higher education institutes
- increased sponsorship programmes
- took on and 'converted' non-technical graduates
- in1987 the HITECC initiative (Higher Introductory Technical and Engineering Conversion Courses) was introduced, which enables school leavers and others with non-science 'A' levels to attend one year conversion courses so they can pursue engineering and technology studies at degree or diploma level.

The Engineering Industry Training Board (EITB), however, are looking for changes to the way engineering is presented in schools and to the type of subject choices school students make which will equip them more closely for a career in engineering and technology.

The construction industry
The need for skilled staff to aid in the construction of the Channel Tunnel led to collaboration between the Training Agency, Kent County Council and Trans-Manche Link (TML), the tunnel contractors. The Local Collaborative Project was set up in January 1986 to examine the likely labour supply and training needs of the project and the impact of the tunnel on local employers. The study also assessed the ability of existing facilities within Kent to meet likely training needs.

The study's major conclusion was that a new skills training centre needs to be established in East Kent offering training in construction skills which will be in shortest supply. The study has, in great detail, predicted labour needs and is a clear example of specific human resource prediction and planning. For instance, it is estimated that at the Tunnel site, the labour force will rise to a peak of 750 by the early months of 1990, tailing off to around 300 by 1993.

To find suitably qualified professional engineers, TML have recruited on a world-wide basis. This included Cairo, Singapore and Malaysia as well as Northern Europe, particularly Belgium. Because of the short-term nature of the project, TML are not re-training non-construction engineers.

The main source of general construction labour has been the Ashford Jobcentre. The Channel Tunnel is competing in a very tight labour market because of the high level of construction activity in the South East, including London Docklands, Gatwick Airport, the completion of the M20, the building of Dartford Bridge as well as major leisure projects.

The message for employers in the 1990s, then, is: skill and labour shortages won't go away. They will need to be planned for, including imaginative use of the various training and re-training programmes which are available, adjustment of recruitment strategies, better, more flexible working conditions and an honest evaluation of the qualifications which are really necessary for the job.

UK anti-discrimination legislation: the influence of the US and Europe in the future

With the coming of the single European market in 1992 it is likely that equal opportunity legislation emanating from Europe will become of increasing importance to the UK. This may signal a move away from the American experience, which has been a source of good practice for the UK in the past.

The US model
The US model has been of fundamental importance for both the structure of anti-discrimination legislation and, to a lesser extent, the interpretation.

Whether this will continue is debatable. The relatively progressive judicial approaches to anti-discrimination law in the US appear to be drying up, and on a number of issues such as equal pay for work of equal value, Europe appears ready to advance beyond the US.

During the Reagan presidency, anti-discrimination legislation and action slowed down. In some instances, legislation was reversed, and Reagan opposed governmental involvement in civil and voting rights issues, including affirmative action. This withdrawal of strong, visible support from anti-discrimination legislation has created a very different civil rights environment in the 1980s.

The position of businesses in this changed atmosphere is one of support for the flexible affirmative action programmes pursued by the Kennedy, Johnson, Nixon, Ford and Carter administrations, and they view the withdrawal or rigidifying of affirmative action legislation with concern. Employers have discovered the following advantages in the system:

- *changing labour market* – as women and minority ethnic groups will form 75 per cent of the US workforce between 1990 and 2000, employers without plans to eliminate barriers will be cut off from this part of the labour force

- *reverse discrimination* – if the relevant legislation is removed, there could be a number of 'reverse discrimination' suits alleging that employers have gone too far with affirmative action

- *good management practice* – the use of goals and targets to track the employment of minority ethnic people and women is consistent with how efficient businesses should be run in every aspect of their operation, eg profits, capital investment, productivity increases and promotion

- *continuity* – employers prefer the uniformity of a single federal regulation instead of having to meet a multiplicity of state and local regulations

- *employee morale and business success* – companies who have made significant progress in hiring minority ethnic groups and women would risk losing skilled employees and certainly suffer a fall in employee morale with a withdrawal of state support from affirmative action programmes.

The UK response
In the UK a greater familiarity with European developments in positive action which go beyond US law could well form the basis of future equality practices.

A more critical approach to US legislation has already begun in the UK. Bob Hepple writes: 'Although discrimination experts often look with envy to the extensive remedial powers of the courts in discrimination cases in the United States, none of them wants the delay, formality and costs associated with American litigation.'[6]

The CRE and EOC have made proposals to remedy this problem. The EOC stated in a consultative paper in March 1989 that discrimination cases took too long, were too complicated and cost too much to be effective. Despite the introduction of the Equal Pay Act, women's wages were still 25 per cent less than men's. Problems in implementing the Act included high costs (up to £10,000 even for simple cases) and lack of precedent-setting in cases which are similar. Joanna Foster, Chair of the EOC, stated that the principles behind the Act did not need reform, but that the implementation did, suggesting 'class actions' on behalf of a number of claimants and a cut in the waiting time for tribunals from an average of 14 to six months.

Another problem in transplanting the US experience to the UK has been the use of the CRE and the EOC as enforcement agencies for a wide range of discriminatory practices. The creation in the UK of these two bodies – the only enforcement technique to be adopted – may have been a mistake. In the US, enforcement techniques (including contract compliance and easier access to courts by individuals) operate in a very different legal context.

The EEC may intervene and recommend a tightening up on effective enforcement of European equality law in member countries.

Future European influence on UK equality legislation

The European influence on the development of UK sex discrimination and equal pay legislation has, until recently, been relatively weak.

The EEC did not influence the initial decision to legislate, nor help determine the structure of UK anti-discriminatory legislation. More recently, however, the EEC has been crucial in confirming and extending the initial UK commitment in a number of areas, most of these lying within the area of sex discrimination and disabilities. There is little EEC legislation or activity on race.

In the UK, sex and race discrimination have tended to be viewed together. As in the US, the use of law to tackle race discrimination preceded the legal attack on sex discrimination and in the UK a policy decision was taken to harmonize the two sets of legislation. It may well be, therefore, that EEC-led activity in sex discrimination precedes or stimulates legislative action in race discrimination.

Whether European influences play a more important role in the future will depend on three main issues:

1 the extent to which non-European factors influence UK policy-making and legal interpretation

2 the success of moves to enforce existing provisions of European law more effectively

3 the degree to which issues of principle and policy can be resolved at the European level.

There has, in the past, been a difference in approach between Europe and the UK. The latter has tended to view EO legislation as a branch of employment law. The influence of European law, with its conception of equality as a fundamental objective of the Treaty may encourage the UK to view equality less as an aspect of industrial relations and more as a basic right. In any case, the approach taken by both sides of UK industry to industrial relations policy is likely to influence the impact of European equality law.

Unions are now starting to bring issues of equality into negotiations with employers, focussing on equal value, parental leave and child care, protective legislation and positive action. The extent to which unions take on the role of implementing equality legislation through collective bargaining will be vital in determining the influence of UK and European law in this area.

European Commission's Agenda for Action
The Agenda for Action programme covers the main areas of equal opportunity practices which the Commission will eventually aim to have in operation in member states. The effectiveness of this depends on the conflict between economic needs (to make money) and social needs (of the next generation's workforce) in each state; and on the role of positive action, the extent of equality legislation and the effectiveness of the enforcement of the law both by Europe and the member state.

Action in the EEC pipeline
The first phase of this programme ran from 1982–85. It was evaluated by the Commission in 1987 in a report which proposed a new five-year programme following up and consolidating actions set out in the 1982–85 programme. These recommendations included the following areas:

Training in equality
This involves informing and training people who are implementing equality legislation, including national lawyers and judges, and the Community Court of Justice. This is being carried out through conferences and ideally also further training for legal and industrial relations practitioners.

Publications on equality are being produced and the Commission is considering the establishment of a Community database on equality.

Monitoring non-compliance
Improving the monitoring of enforcement agencies for non-compliance with existing legislation involves action with member states.

Burden of proof
The Commission is aiming to improve the way of obtaining legal redress by modifying the burden of proof which currently lies on the complainant to establish. This causes problems because the information may be in the hands of the employers, and courts or tribunals are often unwilling to draw inferences from evidence which is presented by the complainant. Modifications are planned in which the burden of proof initially rests with the complainant, but, once discriminatory treatment has been shown, the onus would shift to the respondent to rebut the case.

Sanctions and compensation
Sanctions leading to compensation which should be effective and have a deterrent effect on the employer are planned in discrimination cases.

Sexual harassment
Such legal protection as exists across member states is piecemeal and little pursued. A report by Michael Rubenstein, *The Dignity of Women at Work, a Report on the Problem of Sexual Harassment in the Member States of the European Communities 1987*, forming the first phase of the Commission's response to parliamentary demands for reform, recommends consciousness-raising programmes, documentation of the problem, further research, the publicizing of existing legal non-discrimination rights and support

for complainants, the drawing up of new, clear, legal rights on sexual harassment, and remedies and sanctions.

Revision of protective legislation
The Commission has recently adopted a *Communication on Protective Legislation for Women in the Member States of the European Community*. This reviews the national and international provisions in this area, finding many negative influences on women's employment, eg in the UK, the Health and Safety at Work Act 1974 is excluded from the 1975 Sex Discrimination Act. The Commission has issued a 'reasoned opinion' to the UK stating that section 51 is contrary to the Equal Treatment Directive 76/207. Among the UK's 'anomalous provisions' are the regulations requiring the provision of separate sanitary arrangements for men and women. The Commission's view is that protective legislation should be consistent across sexes and occupational areas. The only exception to this principle should be that permitted by the EEC Equal Treatment Directive covering measures which are strictly necessary to protect the special biological condition of women.

Positive action
The Commission promoted a specific policy of positive action in the first Action Programme which led to the adoption of a Recommendation by the Council on the promotion of positive action for women.

This was in the form of a recommendation rather than a directive to ensure a political commitment from member states. Progress is now being reviewed to assess further action. A booklet, *Positive Action – Equal Opportunities for Women in Employment – a Guide* was produced at the end of 1987 setting out a number of suggestions, all of which can be implemented by UK employers without infringing on the requirements of the Sex Discrimination Act. This builds on the 1984 Recommendation and was introduced because it was realized that 'legal provisions for equal treatment would not in themselves be sufficient to remove existing inequalities affecting women in working life.'

Although member states have begun to introduce positive action measures, they are doing so in widely differing ways. Some concentrate on vocational training or employment measures while others are involved financially in the promotion of positive actions in public or private enterprises. Some states have introduced legislation, while others have issued policy statements.

Maternity protection and maternity leave
There are gaps in existing provision for the protection of women workers during pregnancy and motherhood. There is a need for a clearly stated set of employment rights rather than a limited right under sex discrimination law. The Commission has urged member states to reinforce their national provisions to protect women's job security and eliminate discriminatory effects on recruitment and career advancement, and the Commission itself is laying down guidelines relating to this.

Parental leave and leave for family reasons
This includes paternity leave, periods of leave for fathers at the time of confinement, parental leave, leave to look after young children, compassionate leave and short periods of leave for family reasons.

The Commission backs the sharing of family responsibilities as necessary for equality of opportunity in the labour market. It proposes a Directive on Parental Leave for Family Reasons which would apply to employers in both the public and private sectors, who would be required to provide two types of leave – parental leave and leave for family reasons.

This Directive has not been adopted since it was proposed. However, in 1983 leave for the purposes defined above has become available in all member states except Ireland, the Netherlands and the UK. In Ireland there is a career-break scheme in operation in the public service and the Netherlands are currently drafting legislation on parental leave, but despite intervention by the House of Lords Select Committee on the European Communities and the EOC, the UK Government opposes legal intervention in this area.

Childcare
Again, this provision is variable in member states and does not meet the needs of working parents.

The Commission has no reliable data to formulate policy on day-care facilities for young children, so the Child Care Network has been set up to assemble comparable data on childcare in member states and to make recommendations on necessary facilities.

A major report, *Childcare and Equality of Opportunity* was produced in 1988. It recommended that the European Community and the member states take a number of initiatives, including:

- a framework directive requiring member states to develop publicly-funded childcare services for children at least up to the age of ten with an ultimate objective of ensuring the availability of publicly-funded services for all parents who are employed or in training. The directive should be supplemented by a guide to good practice in childcare services, providing guidelines on how the general objectives might be interpreted and on desirable practices that go beyond what is required by the directive

- a directive establishing a minimum length of maternity leave, parental leave for both partners at the end of maternity leave, and leave for family reasons

- the funding and development of a European programme on childcare and equal opportunities to support studies and action programmes on issues and problems of common interest

- a guide to good practice covering the ways in which fathers may be encouraged and supported to take a more equal share of family responsibilities.

One reason for this initiative is the approach of 1992. Co-ordination of childcare policies is necessary if the concept of a single European market is to work. 'In the present situation, not only are women unable to compete on equal terms in the labour market because of the unequal share of family responsibilities that they carry, but variations between member states are an obstacle to the free movement of labour between member states', the report says.

The UK, however, seems a long way from approving the proposals, with the government maintaining that childcare provision is a matter for private arrangement with no state involvement. The then Junior Health Minister, Edwina Currie, responded to the report thus: 'It is for the parents who go out to work to decide how best to care for their children. If they want or need help in this way they should make the appropriate arrangements and meet the costs.' (Hansard 12.7.88 col. 150).

Systems differ across all member states, and there is concern at Community level that equality law may be affected if the pay or employment opportunities of women, particularly married women, are prejudiced by taxation systems.

The European Parliament raised this concern in 1981 and requested a directive on it. Subsequent action has included:

• an analysis of national systems which showed the diversity across member states

• submission of a memorandum to the Council in December 1984 recommending a system of totally independent taxation for all. (This was approved by the House of Lords Select Committee on the European Communities, the European Parliament and the Economic and Social Committee.)

• discussion of the memorandum at a European conference in 1986

• the current Action Programme requests member states to establish neutral systems which do not act as an employment disincentive for married women.

Community law on equal opportunities operates mainly through the law of the constituent nations. For its success, it needs national courts, practising lawyers and named agencies to be responsible for applying it. Its success in the future will depend on the continuation and development of this and more initiatives in the areas of legal procedures, positive action, taxation, social security and family responsibilities.[7]

The EOC's strategy for the 1990s

The Equal Opportunities Commission, responding to demographic changes and changes in women's expectations and the structure of society, have reviewed and redirected their activities. In *From Policy to Practice, an Equal Opportunities Strategy for the 1990s*[8], the Commission states:

'We shall change from being an organization largely

engaged in securing equal rights for women into a body which can also play a major role in achieving central national economic objectives through the implementation of effective equal opportunities practice.'[8]

This pushing of equal opportunities for women right into the centre of the economic life of the UK is significant. The EOC no longer sees its role as an outsider having to convince the powers that be of women's abilities and potential: these abilities and potential have become central to the prosperity of society.

The EOC's strategy for the 1990s focuses on: enabling women and men to be effective and responsible employees and family members; removing barriers which prevent women from participating in the full range of training opportunities; reducing the difference between men and women's earnings; increasing fiscal and pensions equality and removing disincentives to employment; and developing awareness and acceptance at policy-making and grass roots level that equal opportunities affects all aspects of men's and women's working and non-working lives.

De-regulation and the Employment Bill

The Employment Bill, introduced to parliament at the end of November 1988, proposes the repeal of protective legislation which had been looked upon as outmoded, which could in some cases be looked upon as discriminatory, and which had at times overridden the provisions of the Sex Discrimination Act. If the Bill stays as it is, it will only be possible to override the Sex Discrimination Act where it is necessary to comply with statutory requirements which operate to protect women in relation to pregnancy, maternity and other circumstances involving risks which specifically affect women, eg excessive VDU operation during pregnancy, where medical opinion suggests there may be a risk to the unborn child through radiation. The other two main provisions of the Bill give women the right to statutory redundancy payments up to the same age as men, and allow Chairs of industrial tribunals to run pre-hearing reviews and to ask for a deposit of up to £150 from a complainant who is judged to have no prospect of success or to be bringing a frivolous, vexatious or unreasonable case.

Exclusion clause
The clause which excludes women from certain jobs on health and safety grounds is much narrower than in past legislation. However, it may not go far enough towards meeting the terms of the EEC's Equal Treatment Directive, which narrows exclusion down to situations threatening harm to the mother and child rather than excluding women 'on the ground that public opinion demands that women be given greater protection than men against risks which affect men and women in the same way.'

It similarly promises to fall short of a recent policy statement on *Reproductive and Foetal Hazards* by the US Equal Employment Opportunity Commission which states that exclusion, based on a proved risk of damage to the unborn child, may take place 'but only to the extent necessary to protect employee's offspring from reproductive or foetal hazards . . . It is the Commission's position that, where a reasonable, less discriminatory alternative exists, it must be used.'

If this part of the Bill becomes law, only employer practice will show whether women are being widely excluded from certain types of employment based on the more general 'other circumstances giving rise to risks specifically affecting women.'

Permissible exclusion
Certain provisions from previous protective legislation have been retained. This legislation includes sections from the Public Health Act 1961 and specific industry-based Regulations, eg the Lead Paint Manufacture Regulations 1907.

These provisions allow sex discrimination to take place where a factory occupier employs a woman within four weeks of having a baby; in certain processes involving the use of lead and the mixing of india rubber; where a woman of reproductive capacity has a blood level concentration of lead exceeding the specified limit or is exposed to an excessive dose of ionizing radiation; pregnant women working on aeroplanes or ships; and some educational posts.

Previous restrictions are repeated or extended to both sexes under the Bill, eg clause 7(2) modifies S93 of the Mines and Quarries Act, which prohibited women and young persons from lifting weights which could cause injury by extending the prohibition to men.

Whether this part of the Bill will cause a significant fall in employment standards and safety for women, or whether it will equalize conditions between men and women enabling women to be employed in areas where there were previous, unfounded restrictions, remains to be seen.

Pre-hearing reviews and £150 deposit
There are strong arguments against the review and deposit. The review will take place without full evidence being heard, so will result in the withdrawal of some applications which might have succeeded if the complainant had proceeded. Under the current pre-hearing assessments, 12 per cent of cases where cost warnings have been issued have been ultimately successful. The review will penalize the unrepresented and less articulate complainant, who may be deterred altogether or may increase their costs by taking on legal representation at the review stage. Similarly, the deposit will discourage unemployed and poor litigants while the truly 'vexatious' will still bring complaints. When the Bill becomes law, it may well become more rather than less difficult to use the tribunal system for poorer litigants, thus conflicting with the aim of moving away from complicated litigation procedures. The EOC have pointed out these implications during the consultation period.

The future role of the unions

An Equal Rights Department was established by the TUC at the end of 1988 to work towards more active equal opportunity polices within and outside the TUC. This will spearhead the TUC's campaign for better conditions for women and minority ethnic workers. The 1988 TUC conference felt that the department should be overseen by the existing Equal Rights Committee, which should meet more frequently and be given the same status and authority as other major TUC committees.

For the future, the trade union movement sees equal opportunity issues as focal to collective bargaining as well as elements to be pursued through tribunals. At their 1988 conference, the TUC supported equal pay for work of equal value, backing EEC legislation on the issue. In line with this, the difficulties of using industrial tribunals and the deterrent effect this has on potential claimants was explored (see page 144). The prohibition of contract compliance through the Local Government Act also led to criticism.

Evidence of this proactive approach to equal opportunities has come in a statement on AIDS made by Norman Willis, TUC General Secretary on October 1988. He came out against pre-employment screening for AIDS/HIV infection, and said that the basis of a positive approach to AIDS

> 'is good practice based on treating people fairly at work. We place heavy emphasis on the fact that in most cases good practices developed for all staff should be equally applied to people with AIDS, in exactly the same way as they apply to people with other potentially life threatening diseases such as heart disease or cancer.'

Changing patterns of work and the impact of technology

Moving away from the near certainties of legislation to the wider effects on society, predictions about the future become more uncertain. Changing patterns of work, the impact of technology and their effects on employment practices are all areas of long-term speculation.

This raises a series of questions for personnel practitioners. What will their role be? Will their responsibilities diminish or grow? Where will the main emphasis of their job lie – in refining employment practices, training and re-training or the management of change?

Some of the questions can be answered more easily than others, but overall, one thing is clear: the impact on personnel will be multiple and far-reaching.

They may need to look at their organization as a whole and restructure roles at all levels within that organization. They may be called upon to redefine job roles, often quickly and in an atmosphere of suspicion and anxiety. They will be involved in new methods affecting recruitment, employment practices, training, retraining and flexible working patterns. They will need to offer support and direction to line managers during the implementation process. Above all, their role will focus upon change, upon enabling their organization to change its whole culture and belief system. Personnel will be fundamental to the ease with which organizations in the UK adapt to the employment demands in the late 20th century.

A detailed examination of the impact of technology on wider society belongs in other books. Suffice it to say that the main effect of this has, and will be, an increase in the quality of the manufacturing or service process, and job changes leading to redundancy or retraining needs. However, we can speculate on some of the wider changes and their likely effects on employment and on the groups of people we have considered in this handbook.

The main effect on wider society will probably be to speed up the decentralization of business life. This is happening as much through demands for more flexible working patterns and the high cost of large, central, city locations as it is through the impact of technology. The growth in the use of home-based computers, networks and video links enables this decentralization process to happen. An additional effect will be the continuation of the automation of manufacturing industry and the computerization of service areas.

The decentralization of business life may well include a reduction in the working week, a move away from heavily centrally-based organizations to those which contract out the majority of their work (contract economy – see below), and a growth in self-employment.

This growth in self-employment is documented regularly in press reports:

'Between 1979 and 1981 215,000 more people went into business for themselves, bringing the total in 1981 to over 2 million. It is thought that the increase is continuing at the same rate. And these are just the openly self-employed.

More than 60 per cent are in the service industries, shops, the professions, hotels and catering, with 19 per cent in the building trades and another 12 per cent in farming, forestry and fishing.

The main increase has been in insurance, banking, finance and business services, which expanded by nearly 50 per cent in the two years.

There is still scope for more . . . less than 10 per
cent redundant workers in the 1970s went into self-
employment, and a quarter of them had failed as businesses by 1981'.[9]

'An engineering firm that employs only three people
and operates from a converted terrace cottage has won
a £1 million order from a Turkish oil refinery for automatic loading and moving equipment. All the fabri-
cation work would be contracted out to different manufacturers in the steel-closure hit Scunthorpe area.'[10]

What effect will these changes have on equal opportunity employment policies and practices?

Contract economy
A contract economy is one characterised by a small core of permanent staff, and satellite companies who contract with that core
staff team to carry out specific tasks. It is obvious that a contract
economy will bring about a major redirection, and possible
reduction, in the personnel function.

Central core
The central core will give direction to the organization. It will
cover corporate services, policy and planning functions. The staff
in the central core will need to be highly-skilled and highly-paid.

Contract workers/consultants
The consultants or contract workers need a track record, and
expertise in the specific occupational area, skills in drawing up
proposals, time management and marketing skills and an ability
to deliver.

Role of the personnel department in a contract economy
The personnel department's function in this sort of economy could
change radically. For instance, the recognizable personnel function as it currently exists would operate within the central core.
There would still be the need for recruitment and selection and
conditions of service work; there may be a shift in in-house training needs; there would be a great need for clearly understood
equal opportunities practices in granting contracts and drawing

these contracts up. One advantage of having a smaller central team is that these practices would be easier to communicate and reinforce.

The growth in the granting of contracts would cover both fixed-term and flexible-term contracts. The decision of whether or not to grant these contracts would be that of senior management. Fixed-term contracts would become more common as organizations could no longer afford to commit themselves to expensive specialists for 30 to 40 years; flexible-term contracts would make part-time work more feasible. The drawing up and operation of these contracts may well be moved from personnel into a specialist contract department. The role of personnel, therefore, would be to ensure that these decision and contact points understood the equal opportunities implications of what they were doing. It would need to ensure that employment practices were operating within a legal framework and with a positive action content. It would also need to manage a growing number of personal and portable pension schemes and the implementation of education and training packages, to harmonize the interests of contracted staff and the organization.

Effect on different groups
With a such a radical change in the model of work, can we speculate how the groups which we have looked at in this book will fare?

Minority ethnic groups
If the equal opportunities policies are working effectively in the core team then there should be a proportion of minority ethnic staff within this part of the organization.

This will be important in terms of contract-giving: networks of professional minority ethnic people will develop in the same way as women's networks and old boy networks. This does not suggest favours: what it *does* mean is equal consideration of proposals, whether the approaching company is minority ethnic or white, and a decision made on the grounds of quality.

There may be a problem for minority ethnic groups in building up a track record, which in this context are established through a variety of different jobs and references, ie the Afro-Caribbean, Asian or Chinese firm will have to get those jobs to begin with. There have been many instances of individual and organizational discrimination in this book – it is only the very optimistic who would put a time-scale on such discrimination disappearing. These firms therefore may operate at a disadvantage in a more flexible scenario and be forced to operate in a segmented 'ethnic' market rather than a wider economic context. This would be a repetition of the experience of some small minority ethnic businesses at present and will need active understanding and positive action to overcome.

Women
Women will have a different experience. We have seen that working practices in existing organizations are becoming more flexible to accommodate women returning to work, and that there are a whole variety of flexitime systems (see page 88) which will come into operation. Together with the development of confidence in their own abilities, these will be important in enabling women to be part of the central core of highly-trained, well-paid workers.

In the other half of this working model, women look to benefit greatly from the move towards a contract economy. The greater flexibility of this kind of working will mean that women can fit their working life around the demands of their home life. This, one would hope, will also be true of men, leading towards a more equal balance where both men and women are sharing work and home chores equally.

The disabled
The disabled, also, can benefit from a more flexible working system. Depending on the occupational area they can be home-based, with occasional journeys as necessary to the central location. Modems, computer networks, fax machines and computer based work all offer a real opportunity for disabled people to participate in the workforce to a much greater degree.

Older people
Older people stand to gain from more flexible working patterns. No longer forced to compete for promotion against younger people within the clearly defined career structure of an organization, they will be able to emphasize their strengths – track record, thoroughness, planning, careful implementation – which will become ever more important in a society where the way a job of work is carried out is out of the direct hands of senior management.

Different sexual orientation

A great deal of discrimination against gay men and lesbian women comes from misinformation gathered by the heterosexual workforce about the implications of working with them side by side. With gays, the mistaken understanding of how AIDS is spread, eg through using the same cutlery or cups, and the initial link which has made the disease synonymous with them has intensified antagonistic feelings in the workplace. Eventually this may be countered by anti-discrimination legislation and equal opportunity practices. Until this happens, a contract economy with a large proportion of home working offers the opportunity for gays and lesbians to be judged on achievement rather than sexual orientation.

The future

Speculation apart, the most likely picture for the future is one where a small amount of obvious change is combined with a great deal of what happens at present.

There may, for instance, be a contracts department which handles the contracting out of an increasing amount of work. There may still, however, be a large central organization in which the corporate services – finance, company secretariat and personnel – are housed, together with a policy and senior management team. These staff will need to be serviced. They will need secretaries, they may need catering staff, cleaners, clerks, night watchman. Some people will still need to travel to work, so transport staff will be needed. People will need to service the computers and office furniture, to bring in and look after the plants (in modern offices where a good working environment is essential), and to ensure the office machinery is working efficiently. In other words there will still be a need for clear employment practices but affecting a much broader variety of working patterns.

This may include relocation, a complete change in organizational structure, growing flexibility within working practices, or an emphasis on training, retraining and equality in recruitment practices. With an increasingly complex employment pattern, personnel occupies an ever more central role in ensuring open access for all, regardless of gender, ethnic background, age, disability or sexual orientation.

The future of personnel
What, then, will be the demands on personnel in the future? They will need to have an understanding of equal opportunity policies and of how they should be introduced and implemented. Techniques of introducing and implementing equal opportunity policies will differ with the size, constitution and mode of operation of the organization. They will need the facts about equal opportunities at their fingertips: background knowledge, costings, details of implementation, outcomes. They will need to integrate these policies into existing personnel practices rather than seeing them as additional. They will require an understanding of how to deal with organizational change and the problems and opportunities which this presents, and they will need to involve all staff.

As well as a factual understanding of equal opportunities policies, they will need to see other people's point of view, recognize cost implications, keep both the long-term objectives and short-term view in their vision, and be ready to counteract the perception that equal opportunities are owned by a 'radical group in personnel'. In short, they must be totally convinced that well-developed equal opportunity polices are crucial to their organization's future success.

Personnel will need to be entrepreneurial; to see opportunities and to remain optimistic along what will undoubtedly be a difficult path to travel. At the end of this path, however, will be a more balanced, effective and productive organization and economy reaching into the 21st century. Personnel occupies a central role in enabling this to happen.

References

1 MEAGER NIGEL *and* METCALF HILARY. 'Equal opportunities policies: tactical issues in implementation', Report No 156. London, Institute of Management Studies, 1988.
2 LABOUR RESEARCH DEPARTMENT. 'Bargaining for equality', London, LRD, 1988.
3 EMPLOYMENT DEPARTMENT TRAINING AGENCY. *Skills Bulletin No 5*, London, EDTA, 1988.
4 BUILDING EMPLOYERS CONFEDERATION. *Quarterly Survey of Small Businesses*, 1988.

5   *Evening Standard*, 1 March 1989.
6   HEPPLE, Bob. 'The judicial process in the United Kingdom', *Women, Employment and European equality law*, London, Eclipse Publications, 1987.
7   McCRUDDEN CHRISTOPHER, ed. *Women, employment and European equality law*. London, Eclipse Publications, 1987.
8   EQUAL OPPORTUNITIES COMMISSION. 'From policy to practice: an equal opportunities strategy for the 1990s.' London, EOC, 1988.
9   *Guardian*, 6 August 1983.
10 *Daily Telegraph*, 7 July 1983.

Resources

Ashridge Management College
Berkhamsted
Herts HP4 1NS
044 284–3491
Runs management courses including courses on flexible working patterns.

Association of Metropolitan
Authorities (AMA)
36 Old Queen Street
London SW1
071–930 9861

Centre for Personnel Research
and Enterprise Development
The City University Business
School
Northampton Square
London EC1V 0HB
071–253 4399
Source of research into women and employment.

Commission for Racial Equality
Elliot House
10–12 Allington Street
London SW1 5EH
071–828 7022

Department of Education for
Northern Ireland
Rathgael House
Balloo Road
Bangor
Co. Down BT19 2PR
0247–66311

Department of Education and
Science (DES)
Elizabeth House
York Road
London SE1 7PH
081–943 9885/0888

Department of Employment
Caxton House
Tothill Street
London SW1H 9NF
071–273 5524

Equal Opportunities Commission
Overseas House
Quay Street
Manchester M3 3HN
061–833 9244

Fullemploy Consultancy
County House
190 Great Dover Street
London SE1 4YB
071–378 1774
Consultants on race equality in employment practices.

Further Education Unit (FEU)
Elizabeth House
York Road
London SE1 7PH
071–934 9413
Concerned that the further education system should provide effective support for employees in inner cities.

Industrial Society
3 Carlton House Terrace
London SW19 5DG
071–839 4300
Runs training courses, produces videos and publications covering a wide range of management training courses including some on equal opportunities.

Institute of Directors
116 Pall Mall
London SW1Y 5ED
071–839 1233
Runs occasional courses on patterns of women's work

Institute of Personnel Management
IPM House
Camp Road
Wimbledon
London SW19 4UX
081–946 9100

Learning from Experience Trust (LET)

Regent's College
Regent's Park
London NW1 4NS
071–487 7405
An educational charity established to develop ways in which people can make maximum use of their knowledge and skills, however they acquired them.

Local Government Training Board
Arndale House
Arndale Centre
Luton LU1 2TS
0582–451166
Directory of race relations and equal opportunities trainers and training materials.

Medical Aids Centre
British Red Cross Society
76 Clarendon Road
Leicester LE2 3AD
0533–700747
Holds details of Centres which can give advice on non-medical aids needed by the disabled worker to do a particular job.

MSF (Manufacturing, Science, Finance Union)
79 Camden Road
London NW1 9ES
071–267 4422

National Economic Development Office
Millbank Tower
Millbank
London SW1P 4QX
071–217 4000

NCVQ (National Council for Vocational Qualifications)

222 Euston Road
London NW1 2BZ
071-387 9898

New Ways to Work
309 Upper Street
London N1 2TY
Organization researching and
promoting the advantages of job-
sharing and other flexible ways of
working.

Open College
101 Wigmore Street
London W1H 9AA
071-935 8088

Open University
Walton Hall
Milton Keynes MK7 6AA

The Pathway Employment Service
169a City Road
Cardiff CF2 3JB
0222-482072
Puts employers in touch with
suitable mentally handicapped
people in terms of recruitment and
provides financial assistance.

Roffey Park College
Forest Road
Horsham
West Sussex RH12 4TD
029 383-644
Runs management development
programmes for women.

Royal Association for Disability
and Rehabilitation (RADAR)
25 Mortimer Street
London W1N 8AB
071-637 5400
Advice on adaptations to
premises, transport solutions etc.
which may be needed to recruit or

retain a disabled worker.
Publishes the 'Employers Guide
to Disabilities'.

Royal National Institute for the
Blind
224 Great Portland Street
London W1N 6AA
071-388 1266

Royal National Institute for the
Deaf
195 Gower Street
London
WC1E 6AH
071-387 8033

Scottish Education Department
New St Andrews House
St James Centre
Edinburgh EH1 3SY
031-556 8400

Training Agency
Moorfoot
Sheffield S1 4PQ
0742-703342
Funders of vocational training in
the UK.

Unemployment Unit
9 Poland Street
London W1V 3DG
Provides research and publicity
surrounding issues of
unemployment.

Unit for the Development of
Adult Continuing Education
(UDACE)
Christopher House
Leicester LE2 0QS
0533-542645
A DES funded unit aiming to
develop a broad, accessible range
of learning opportunities for
adults.

University of London
CHES/DEAPSIE
2 Taviton Street
London WC1H 0BT
071–380 0519
or

57 Gordon Square
London WC1
071–636 1500
Video materials and training
packages on racism awareness

Welsh (Education) Office
Cathays Park
Cardiff CF1 3NQ
0222–28066

Publications

Labour Market Quarterly Report
produced by Employment Department Training Agency
Labour Market Information Service
Moorfoot
Sheffield S1 4PQ
0742–704075
Information on employment trends, changes in the labour market and
the role of training

Women and Training News
GLOSCAT
Oxtalls Lane
Gloucester GL2 9HW

Skills Bulletin
produced by Employment Department Training Agency
Moorfoot
Sheffield S1 4PQ
0742–703149/703639
Focuses on the need for human resource planning, forecasts skills
shortages and mismatches

Publishers

Fullemploy Publications
County House
190 Great Dover Street
London SE1 4YB
071–378 1774
Publishers of text and video-based race equality training materials.

Industrial Relations Services
18–20 Highbury Place
London N5 1QP
071–359 4000
Publishers of the 'Equal Opportunities Review' reporting on
developments in equal opportunities practices, procedures and
legislation covering minority ethnic groups, women, the disabled, those
of different sexual orientation and age.

NEDO Books
Millbank Tower
Millbank
London
SW1P 4QX

Appendix 1

IPM Equal Opportunities Code

The Institute of Personnel Management have produced 'The IPM Equal Opportunities Code' as a guide to personnel managers. As well as covering legal and implementation aspects, the role of the personnel manager is discussed in terms of the knowledge necessary to bring a focus to equal opportunities policies and integrate them into other employment practices. Recommendations include a knowledge of the three basic Acts which define the legal aspects of equal opportunity practices, a knowledge of the important cases on various issues of principle which have been decided, familiarity with the two 'statutory' codes (EOC and CRE) and a knowledge of where to go for information and advice. Available from the Equal Opportunities Department, IPM, IPM House, Camp Road, Wimbledon, London SW19 4UX.

Appendix 2

IPM Code on Occupational Testing

This code, drawn together by IPM, the British Psychological Society, the CRE and the EOC aims to promote good practice in the selection, administration and interpretation of occupational tests. It was developed to give guidance on avoiding unfair bias in the use of these tests and covers areas such as:

What kinds of occupational tests exist? When should they be used? What practical issues are involved in their use? How are occupational tests used to make employment decisions? How should their use be monitored and evaluated?

The IPM Code on Occupational Testing is available from the Institute of Personnel Management at the address in the resources section.

Appendix 3

Awareness training

Racism awareness training
In the years since mass immigration of minority ethnic groups first started in the late 1940s, official policy towards race has passed through three different broad phases.

1 *'colour blindness'*
   Immigrants and their children were officially treated no differently from anyone else. The signs of racism such as slogans, eg 'no dogs or blacks', were ignored.

2 *control of numbers*
   In response to perceived tension in working class areas, and the Notting Hill riots in the 1950s, the Commonwealth Immigrants Act was passed in 1962 in an attempt to control the numbers of immigrants.

3 *'integration' and cultural pluralism*
   Labour tried to address the pervasive background of racial discrimination which was beginning to show. Roy Jenkins, Home Secretary in the 1966–70 Wilson government proposed a strategy which offered 'equal opportunity, accompanied by cultural diversity, in an atmosphere of mutual tolerance.'
   The 1968 Race Relations Act strengthened a weak Race Relations Act (1965) by enlarging the scope from public places to employment and housing, and empowered a Race Relations Board to investigate discrimination.
   However, further studies showed that subtle and widespread discrimination remained. The 1976 Race Relations Act reflected concern that racism was often powerfully expressed

below the surface. It recognized that equal opportunities had to be promoted rather than allowed to emerge over time and the CRE was set up and given responsibility for taking the lead on this.

In the mid 1970s the atmosphere shifted from an assimilationist and integrationist stance which assumed a coherent society to one promoted by Peter Newsam (later chair of the CRE) which channelled extra resources to minority ethnic groups. The eradication of racism had become a legitimate object of policy. Increasingly the minority ethnic communities were seen as distinct from each other and potentially as the victims of white society.

This recognition – that the different ethnic communities are very different, and are very oppressed; that their cultures are as important to them as majority cultures are to the majority and should be understood by the white community; and that part of the job of understanding is an appreciation of white racism rooted in the past, formed the background to racism awareness training.

Racism awareness training (RAT) was developed in the US and given voice by Judith Katz in *Systematic Handbook of Exercises for the Re-education of White People with Respect to Attitudes and Behaviourisms* (1976).

It became popular in the 1980s when some institutions used it as a tool to bring about change in attitudes amongst their staff. This was against a background described by Robin Cohen, executive director of the Centre for Research in Ethnic Relations at Warwick.

'The race relations legislation and initiatives have been quite effective in changing social behaviour. It may mean people are learning something: or that feelings are hidden – there, but seen to be forbidden.'

RAT is sometimes delivered by black trainers for black participants, sometimes to racially mixed groups, sometimes by black trainers for white participants. It developed to explore the conflict between black and white people, and the terminology used reflects this. The use of all black and all white groups is to create a 'safe' environment in which participants can explore their feelings about racism. The aim of RAT for black people is to help them understand the historical factors which have led to racism and to develop a black consciousness to use as a basis for personal growth and development.

For white people, it aims to help them become aware of themselves as white people, and to recognize the history of their negative and often oppressive relationships with black people.

Typical comments from individuals participating in racism awareness courses on changes in their attitudes have been:

> 'owning up to my identity and not making myself feel inferior to anybody. And also making people know who I am and respect me for that.' (Black workshop)

> 'I became very aware of my ignorance and lack of understanding of the problem – (now) I am less ignorant and understand better.' (White workshop)[1]

The assumption that racism is a white problem which all white people have has, however, become the focus of a vigorous debate. Part of that debate focuses on whether RAT expunges guilt or encourages it to grow.

The report (which is still to be published) on the murder of an Asian pupil by a white pupil at Burnage School, Manchester in 1986, produced by a multi-ethnic inquiry team, criticized the use and ideology of racism awareness training in the school. It argued that the effect of imposing policies on white working class children and parents, who themselves feel marginalized from society, was to increase their resentment and to give it a racial focus.[2]

> 'It has reinforced the guilt of many well-meaning whites and has paralyzed them when any issue of race arises, or has taught others to bury their racism without in any way changing their attitude.'

Gus John (assistant education officer at ILEA, and a veteran of community relations) stated:

> 'one of the things many anti-racist policies lack is any appreciation that you are not dealing with an undiffer-

entiated mass of white people. I refuse to accept that
white people are irredeemably racist.'

Sexism awareness training
Sexism awareness training, in the context of employment, is made
up of a variety of different strands. These include assertiveness
training, self-development, networking, and the use of mentors
and role models. It covers the acquisition both of skills which
enable women to be effective at work, and of those which help
them to develop a political awareness about how things are
achieved within an organization.

1   assertiveness training
The essence of assertive behaviour is equality. 'Assertive communication is usually defined as clear, honest and direct. It is
the ability to express one's need, opinions, feelings and wishes
in an appropriate manner without violating the rights of the
other person.'[3]

Being assertive is not being aggressive. It is understanding
oneself and communicating successfully with others. It involves
coping with other people's attitudes and opinions, and also
with the self-negating attitudes which may originate from
within. Techniques include being able to make clear requests,
using body language as well as voice; saying 'no' to others'
requests when it is difficult to do so; disagreeing without either
humiliating the other person or stepping down yourself;
expressing feelings and handling criticism.

2   self-development
Individuals are encouraged to take personal responsibility for
their own development. Self-development allows women to
broaden their understanding of themselves and the effect they
have on others. It allows them to move from the personal to
organizational and managerial concepts.

3   networking
The need for a wide range of contacts is part of the increasing
political awareness amongst women. An analogy with the 'old
boys' network is often made. Many organizations are now
actively encouraging and supporting women's networks.

4   *mentoring and role models*
Mentoring is the use of a top-management person as a role model. A problem can be finding enough female role models, but this problem assumes that role models are swallowed whole and therefore have to be women. In fact it is perfectly possible to use the best aspects of different individuals, and whether the models are men or women becomes irrelevant.

Mixed versus women only groups
Single sex groups provide an environment in which women seem more prepared to take risks, and it is only by taking risks that personal development occurs.

Increasingly, development programmes are offered in different forms: for instance women-only, modular, mixed residential, so that women and organizations may choose the most appropriate methods. Some women, for example, might choose to learn management techniques through distance learning such as that offered by the Open University, to develop personal awareness by joining a network and to increase their skills by attending short modular programmes. It is important, however, that women's management training is kept close to and involved with mainstream management development.[4]

Male awareness training
Although less established than racism awareness training, male awareness training (MAT) follows similar patterns in practice and in implementation. Male awareness training aims to give males the opportunity to explore their own sexism, to understand how this evolved and what processes ensure that it continues, unless some fundamental changes take place.

Evidence suggests that boys do not communicate in the same way, or to the same extent as girls. Males tend to be more competitive and suppress emotions. One of the basic levels of MAT, if males are to behave in an anti-sexist way in what is an unequal society, is to recognize that such characteristics, for instance appearing tough and resolute, are products of conditioning, not innate.

Implementation of equal opportunities policies
This conditioning may cause problems when it comes to implementing equal opportunity policies. Local authorities have often

been the first to introduce equal opportunity policies, to recognize the problem, and to develop principles and experience in the delivery of male awareness training. For instance, they have discovered through practice that the male trainers involved must have a personal commitment to the concept of equal opportunities, that consultations with relevant women's groups within the authority should take place to ensure the MAT's aims and objectives are understood, and that the training programme is on-going, and not a series of 'one offs'.[5]

1   *male trainers*
The argument goes that the trainers should be male so that the male participants can explore their sexism in a secure situation. It also encourages the men to take responsibility for changing their attitudes. They must discover and understand the conditioning they have been subjected to, supported by the male trainers.

2   *consultations with women's groups*
Often women's groups feel anxious that if men are involved in training other men, inequalities and attitudes are likely to be perpetuated rather than changed. But MAT is more than getting males to work in an anti-sexist way: it is aimed at developing an understanding of why they are sexist.

3   *ongoing training*
Once MAT becomes an accepted part of mainstream training, consideration needs to be given to its future development, its implementation within departmental structures, and whether it should be compulsory for all males to participate.
MAT should work as part of an equal opportunities policy and as such has to be supported by senior management. Once this support is given, key officers can be instructed to attend a Male Awareness Training course. Once a pilot course has been run, acceptance and development of a MAT programme becomes easier, and voluntary participation, which produces better results, should be the chosen method of recruitment. The next developmental stage should be for groups to co-operate to create and develop agreed anti-sexist working strategies and practice which should be monitored, evaluated and reviewed.

References

1 LEWISHAM RACISM AWARENESS TRAINING UNIT. *Report 1984–87, the early years.*
2 LLOYD JOHN. 'The guilt that dares not speak its name', *Financial Times*, 21 May 1988.
3 DICKSON ANNE. 'Assertiveness training at work'. *Gender and work: a guide to materials for women and men in organizations* edited by Tom Boydell and Mike Pedler. London, Manpower Services Commission, 1988.
4 HAMMOND VALERIE. 'Management development for women'. *ibid.*
5 LANGFORD JOHN. 'Males awareness training'. *Women and Training News* Issue 24, Autumn 1986.

Index